Ray Melius

Android Application Development

Practical Guide and Easy Learning

Tutorial

Ray is a Senior Software Engineer. He has been in IT field for 30 years with broad experience in different industries, private and government organizations, and scientific institutions.
He holds Master's degree in Computer Science.

I want to thank my loving wife

P. Lee for her great support

Table of Contents

TABLE OF FIGURES

Preface

Preface

Preface

Android is the first open source and free mobile platform. It offers unlimited opportunities for mobile application developers. Eclipse is the most explored integrated development environment (IDE) for Java programmers. Since Android applications are Java based, it naturally becomes the preferred IDE for Android applications too. Android Application Development uses Eclipse plus ADT plugin as a basic tool for development.

We consider that the fast and easiest way of learning is by examples. Every new concept is illustrated by a simple demo application. I this way the readers first "feel and see" the concept in a real running app even before they completely understand it. The full explanation and knowledge comes after that.

Who This Book Is For

This book is meant for both beginners and intermediate application developers who would like to come up quickly to Android development using the Android Development Tools Bundle.

The main method is first to build a running example that illustrates some concept and next we explain the programming concept through that example.

Preface
What You Will Learn

- How to install, configure and to use the most popular ADT (Android Development Tools) for Android development
- The basics of Android application development are explained systematic trough working applications. You may follow the explanations from the book or just download, install the project and run the application.
- Useful tips and tricks for creating spectacular applications.
- How to troubleshoot and debug Android applications using ADT. It includes a list of common errors and their resolutions.
- The complete project published on Google Play and instructions how to prepare and publish your application.

How To Read This Book

It is structured in such a way so the learning process be intuitive and fast. The hyperlinks pointing to main concepts make navigation between different parts of the book easy.

The reader may follow step-by-step instructions illustrated by screenshots or download and run the demo app and later follow the explanations. After finishing the part I you may skip Application Fundamentals and choose topics in random order and use hyperlinks for quick reference.

Preface
Downloading The Code

The DEMO projects for this book are available for download from

http://ultinf.com/downloads/android-projects/

Part I:
Getting Started

ICON KEY

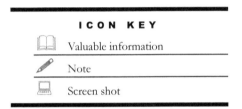

📖	Valuable information
✎	Note
💻	Screen shot

1. Creating your First Application

Setting up the ADT Bundle

Everything that you need for developing Android applications is included in ADT (Android Development Tools) Bundle: Eclipse plus ADT plugin, Android SDK and Platform Tools. Instead of installing them separately, go to http://developer.android.com/sdk/index.html#download and download the latest ADT Bundle. Unpack the ZIP file and save it to an appropriate directory: <ADT>. Open the <ADT>/eclipse directory and launch **eclipse**.

Using **Window > SDK Manager** download/update the latest SDK tools and platforms:

Android SDK Tools, Android SDK Platform-tools, Android SDK Build-tools, Android 4.4.2 (API 19): [ARM EABI System Image, Google APIs (ARM System Image)], Android 2.3.3 (API 10): [SDK Platform, Google APIs], Extras:[Android Support Library, Google Play Services]

Figure 1 : Updating the latest SDK tools and platforms

To check installation see Installation details

> At the time of writing this book, the last API version is Android L (API20 L), still in Preview mode. That is why we prefer more common API 19 (Android 4.4.2) and (Android 4.4.W (API 20) for which more tools are available. Of course, the reader may install and experiment with more packages.

> There is a new Android development environment (Android Studio): based on IntelliJ IDEA: For installation instructions see: http://developer.android.com/sdk/installing/studio.ht ml#Updating

Since at the time of writing this book it is in BETA version, we will use ADT (Eclipse) as a main tool.

Creating Skeleton Project

The skeleton project is an empty "Hello world" project. In all the examples hereafter, we will add java classes to that basic project.

Create New Android Application Project with empty Activity:

1. Click **New** in the toolbar or select from top menu **File>New**
2. In the context menu that appears, open the **Android** folder, select **Android Application Project**, and click **Next**.

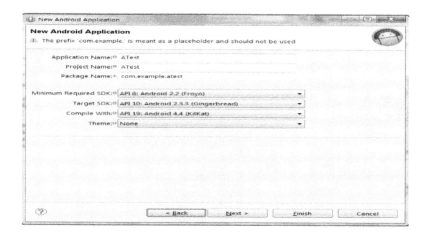

Figure 2:The New Android App Project wizard in Eclipse

3. Fill in the form: For example for **ApplicationName** use ATest.
   The next three fields will be filled by default with the same name:

   a. **Application Name**: ATest

   b. **Project Name** is the name of your project directory and the name visible in Eclipse.

   c. **Package Name** is the package namespace for your application

4. Press **Next**

5. On **New Android Application** leave the check boxes by default. Make sure that 'Create Activity' is checked and press **Next.**

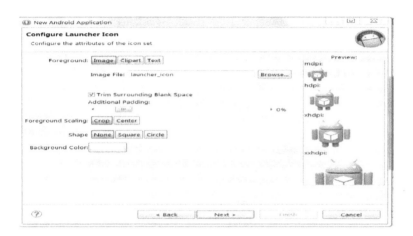

6. On **Configure Launcher Icon** screen you may select new icon. Select default for now and press **Next**

7. On Create Activity screen select Empty Activity and press Next

8. On the next screen for Activity **Name,** use ATestActivity. The next fields (in the case of Empty Activity only one) automatically are filed up with names, containing ATest and press **Finish.**

9. After a while **Eclipse** creates automatically the project with various folders and source files:

🖥 *Figure 3: Final Project*

For detailed explanation of most significant files and folders see App Resources . For now, let's see how to execute this application. If you have just installed your ADT, you need to create an AVD device for testing. Otherwise, you may go directly to next section: Running the skeleton project.

Install and run AVD device:

The cycle of developing an application includes many re-executions and debugging the code. That is why we need a simulator on which we can run and debug it. Only at the final stage we install and run the app on a real Android device.

From top menu select Window > Android Virtual Device Manager > New

- In the Android Virtual Device Manager panel, click **New**.
- Fill in the details for the AVD. Give it a name, a platform target, an SD card size, and a skin (HVGA is default).
- Click **Create AVD**.

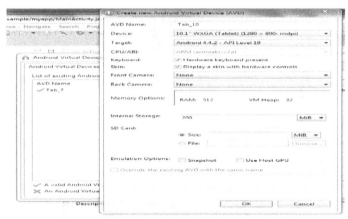

-
- Select Memory Options: **RAM** 512, **VM Heap**: 32, choose resolution you like (.e.g. 480 x 800) and other options like on the screenshots:

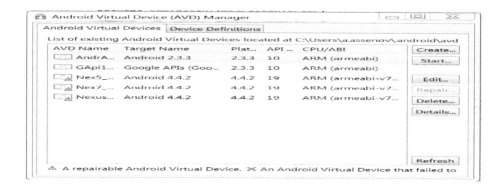

Figure 4: Creating of AVD

After creating a virtual device, select it from Android Virtual Device

Manager and type **Start** in order to run it:

After a while, you should see something like this:

Figure 5: Running instance of AVD

For more options and info about AVD see AVD –Telnet access and
Testing of an APK on Simulator

Running the Skeleton Project

To run the Application:

- Right-click on project name (ATest) in Package Explorer (Left pane).
- From the context menu select: Run As > Android Application and click OK.
- After application loads you should see the "Hello world" screen on virtual device:

Figure 6: The First App

2. Graphical User Interface

All graphical user interface (GUI) components are contained in layouts. In Eclipse, when you open a layout file, you are first shown the Graphical Layout editor. It helps you build your layout using WYSWYG tools. Every action in Graphical Layout editor is recorded to corresponding xml file. The GUI builder could in principle, generate Java code instead of XML. Most everything you do using XML layout files can be achieved through Java code. The challenge is re-building and re-using of view definitions – that is far simpler if the data is in a structured format like XML than in a programming language.

We will demonstrate how to use GUI components via the following working example.

DEMO APP: Length Converter

We are going to build a simple **interactive** application that converts lengths measured in meters (SI metric system) to feet (American metric system) and vice versa. During the process of creation you will learn how to add simple GUI elements and attach onClick events to them. First, we will build a simple Length Converter app.

The running application should look like this:

🖥 *Figure 7: Length Converter App*

Later we will enhance it with more functionality to a project called Metric
Converter. It is published on Google Play and may be downloaded free.

To start: Create a skeleton project with application name
LengthConverter, package and project name com.ultinf.LengthConverter,
and activity name ConvertLengthActivity.

Add GUI elements to your layout

Select the res/layout/activity_convert_length.xml file and click on
Graphical Layout. This editor allows you to create the WYSWYG layout
via drag and drop or via the XML source code.

Right-click on the existing Hello World! text object. Select Delete from
the popup menu to remove that object.

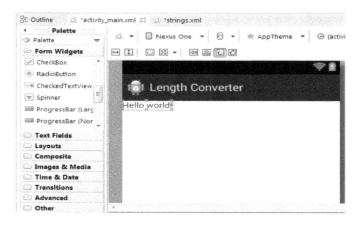

Afterwards select the **Form Widgets** section in the **Palette** and drag

a **Medium Text** widget into the layout. Click on the **Text Fields** section

header in the **Palette** to see all text fields and locate the **Number**

(Decimal). Drag the **Number (Decimal)** field to the right of **Medium**

Text widget to create a decimal number input field. Repeat the two

actions again on the second row. Drag another **Medium Text** widget

below the first one and another **Number (Decimal)** field. While dragging

you will see aligning arrows that help to align the GUI elements.

Finally, from **Form Widgets select Button** widget and align it below the

second **Number (Decimal)** field. You should see something like the

following screenshot. New versions of ADT change the templates, so

your screen might look slightly different.

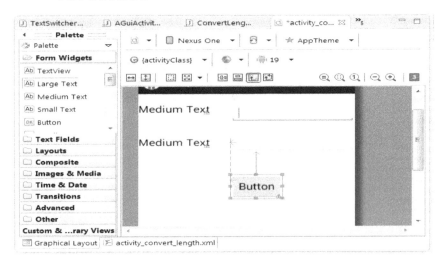

🖥 *Figure 8: GUI Palette*

Edit GUI elements properties

We can change attributes of a GUI element via the

Eclipse **Properties** menu from Structure > Outline pane or via the context

menu by right-clicking on a GUI element. If you don't see Outline

window, select it from **Windows > Show View > Outline**.

You can also change properties of a GUI element directly in the XML file,

which is typical faster if you have some experience with xml.

Here we will use the Graphical Layout editor, which provides WYSWYG

support. It provides also content assists via the Ctrl+Space shortcut. Use

a right-click on editText1 text field in ActivityConvertLength.xml in

Graphical Layout. On the right Properties Pane find OnClick property and

add to the right onClick event. Right-click on editText2 text field and

repeat the operation. We will use the onClick event to indicate that the

user wants to write a value in that field. The corresponding field will be

cleared in order to receive the calculated value.

✎ Note: When using existing projects, always check that the API version of the project correspond to the API version of the Graphical Layout (see Graphical Layout).

Create attributes

Using a right-click on res/values/styles from Package explorer invoke

📖 *Figure 9: Attributes and Styles*

Assign user defined attributes

In order to assign lcColor as a background color to ActivityConvertLength Layout:

Right-click on an empty space in Graphical Layout mode, then select Edit Background. Select Color and then select lcColor in the dialog.

Figure 10: User defined attributes

Use a right-click on textView1 to assign the Meter (m) String attribute to its text property. Assign to textView2 Foot (ft) String attribute to its text property. Switching to xml layout you will see the following code generated:

```
<RelativeLayout
xmlns:android="http://schemas.android.com/apk/res/android"
    xmlns:tools="http://schemas.android.com/tools"
    android:layout_width="match_parent"
    android:layout_height="match_parent"
    tools:context="${packageName}.${activityClass}" >

    <TextView
        android:id="@+id/textView1"
        android:layout_width="wrap_content"
        android:layout_height="wrap_content"
        android:layout_alignParentLeft="true"
        android:layout_alignParentTop="true"
        android:layout_marginTop="20dp"
        android:text="Meter (m)"

android:textAppearance="?android:attr/textAppearanceMedium" />

    <EditText
        android:id="@+id/editText1"
        android:layout_width="wrap_content"
        android:layout_height="wrap_content"
        android:layout_alignLeft="@+id/editText2"
        android:layout_alignTop="@+id/textView1"
```

```
                    android:ems="10"
                    android:inputType="numberDecimal"
                    android:onClick="onClick" >

                <requestFocus />
            </EditText>

            <TextView
                    android:id="@+id/textView2"
                    android:layout_width="wrap_content"
                    android:layout_height="wrap_content"
                    android:layout_alignParentLeft="true"
                    android:layout_below="@+id/editText1"
                    android:layout_marginTop="29dp"
                    android:text="Foot (ft)"

    android:textAppearance="?android:attr/textAppearanceMedium" />

            <EditText
                    android:id="@+id/editText2"
                    android:layout_width="wrap_content"
                    android:layout_height="wrap_content"
                    android:layout_alignBaseline="@+id/textView2"
                    android:layout_alignBottom="@+id/textView2"
                    android:layout_marginLeft="30dp"
                    android:layout_toRightOf="@+id/textView2"
                    android:ems="10"
                    android:inputType="numberDecimal"
                    android:onClick="onClick" />

            <Button
                    android:id="@+id/button1"
                    android:layout_width="wrap_content"
                    android:layout_height="wrap_content"
                    android:layout_alignLeft="@+id/editText2"
                    android:layout_below="@+id/editText2"
                    android:layout_marginTop="52dp"
                    android:onClick="onClick"
                    android:text="Convert" />

        </RelativeLayout>
```

Change the activity code

The Android project wizard created the
corresponding ConvertLengthActivity class for your activity code.
Let's start adding code to the generated class.

First, we want to add a EditText member: **private EditText** txtMetric;

We see the error icon next to that line. If we left-click on it, the Android
Lint presents a list of suggestions to resolve the problem:

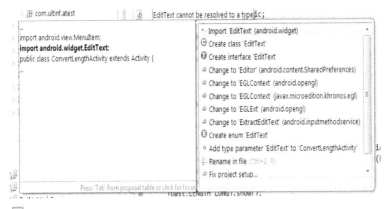

Figure 11: List of suggestions to resolve the problem

Select and click on the first and obvious one: **Import 'EditText'**. Eclipse inserts the necessary import android.widget.EditText;

In onCreate() we would like to initiate these two objects:

```
protected void onCreate(Bundle savedInstanceState) {
            super.onCreate(savedInstanceState);

        setContentView(R.layout.activity_convert_length);
                txtMetric =    (EditText)
findViewById(R.id.editText1);
                txtUSMetric = (EditText)
findViewById(R.id.editText2);
        }
```

Afterwards we add onClick() event handler. Since we added to all GUI elements the same event name - onClick we check for their ID via view.getId() in order to take corresponding actions:

```
public void onClick(View view) {
    switch (view.getId()) {
    case R.id.editText1:
        txtUSMetric.setText("");
        break;
```

```
case R.id.editText2:
        txtMetric.setText("");
        break;

case R.id.button1:
            ...
    }
}
```

Here is the complete code snippet for ConvertLengthActivity

class:

```
package com.ultinf.lengthconverter;

import com.ultinf.lengthconverter.R;

import android.app.Activity;
import android.os.Bundle;
import android.view.View;
import android.widget.Button;
import android.widget.EditText;
import android.widget.Toast;

public class ConvertLengthActivity extends Activity {
private EditText txtMetric;
private EditText txtUSMetric;
@Override
protected void onCreate(Bundle savedInstanceState) {
        super.onCreate(savedInstanceState);
        setContentView(R.layout.activity_convert_length);
        txtMetric =   (EditText) findViewById(R.id.editText1);
        txtUSMetric = (EditText) findViewById(R.id.editText2);
}

// "OnClick" event handler of the text fields and button
public void onClick(View view) {
        double inpVal, outVal;
    switch (view.getId()) {
    case R.id.editText1:
        txtUSMetric.setText("");
      break;

    case R.id.editText2:
            txtMetric.setText("");
            break;

    case R.id.button1:
        if ( ((txtMetric.getText().length() == 0) &&
(txtUSMetric.getText().length() == 0)) ||
            ((txtMetric.getText().length() != 0) &&
(txtUSMetric.getText().length() != 0)))
            {
            Toast.makeText(this, "Please enter a valid
number in one of the fields ",
                Toast.LENGTH_LONG).show();
            txtUSMetric.setText("");
            txtMetric.setText("");
```

```
            return;
         }
      if ( (txtMetric.getText().length() == 0) )
         {
             inpVal =
Double.parseDouble(txtUSMetric.getText().toString());
               outVal = 0.3048 * inpVal ;
               txtMetric.setText(String.valueOf(outVal));
         }
      else
         {
             inpVal =
Double.parseDouble(txtMetric.getText().toString());
               outVal = 3.281 * inpVal ;

txtUSMetric.setText(String.valueOf(outVal));
         }
      break;
      }
   }
}
```

Build and run the application.

DEMO APP: Metric Converter - published on Google Play

We are going to add more functionality to the previous example. It leads to an app – Metric Converter, which can be free downloaded and installed from Google Play. It is available at the following URL:

https://play.google.com/store/apps/details?id=com.ultinf.metricconverter

Refactoring

First, we rename the previous project to MetricConverter. We should refactor the two packages in **src** and **gen** folders:

In Package Explorer pane right-click on **src >**

com.ultinf.lengthconverter and from context menu select

Refactor>Rename. Set the new name: com.ultinf.metricconverter.

Repeat the same procedure with **gen > com.ultinf.lengthconverter**

Change the package name of Manifest file to com.ultinf.metricconverter

Figure 12: List of suggestions to resolve the problem

For more info, see Refactoring.

You need to do twice **Project > Clean** from main menu in order R.java resource file to be properly generated. Rename in the same way `ConvertLengthActivity` to `ConvertMetricsActivity`.

Figure 13: Rename Package

Add new radio group

From Form Widgets drag a RadioGroup widget onto Layout and position it above Convert button. Inside there are three RadioButtons:

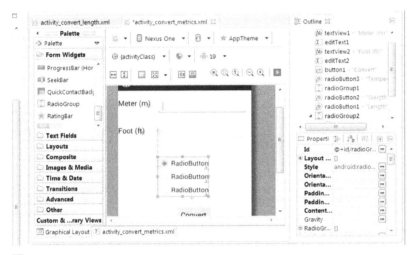

Figure 14: Add new Radio Group

Right-click on RadioButtons1-3 and from context menu select Edit Text and change the names to Length, Weight and Temperature.

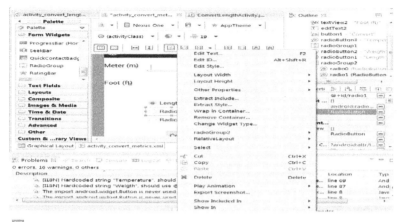

📃 *Figure 15: Changing of text names*

Right-click on RadioGroup and select from Properties pane Orientation:
Horizontal.

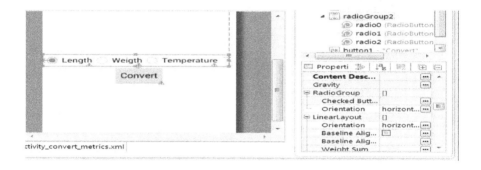

📃 *Figure 16: Horizontal alignment*

Use a right-click on radio0 field in ActivityConvertMetric.xml in Graphical
Layout. On the right Properties Pane find OnClick property and add to the
right onClick event. Right-click on radio1,2 fields and repeat the
operation.

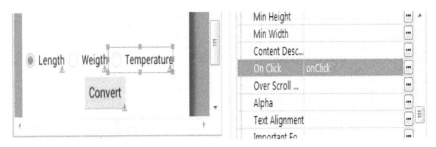

🖥 *Figure 17: onClick Property*

Right-click on Convert button and change the onClick event to onCalc.

We want to have a special event handler for calculating values. Switch to xml layout to check the code generated:

```xml
<RelativeLayout
xmlns:android="http://schemas.android.com/apk/res/android"
    xmlns:tools="http://schemas.android.com/tools"
    android:layout_width="fill_parent"
    android:layout_height="fill_parent"
    android:background="@color/mcColor"
    tools:context="${packageName}.${activityClass}" >

    <TextView
        android:id="@+id/textView1"
        android:layout_width="wrap_content"
        android:layout_height="wrap_content"
        android:layout_alignParentLeft="true"
        android:layout_alignParentTop="true"
        android:layout_marginTop="20dp"
        android:text="Meter (m)"

android:textAppearance="?android:attr/textAppearanceMedium" />

    <EditText
        android:id="@+id/editText1"
        android:layout_width="wrap_content"
        android:layout_height="wrap_content"
        android:layout_alignLeft="@+id/editText2"
        android:layout_alignTop="@+id/textView1"
        android:ems="10"
        android:inputType="numberDecimal"
        android:onClick="onClick" >

        <requestFocus />
    </EditText>

    <TextView
        android:id="@+id/textView2"
        android:layout_width="wrap_content"
        android:layout_height="wrap_content"
        android:layout_alignParentLeft="true"
        android:layout_below="@+id/editText1"
```

```
            android:layout_marginTop="30dp"
            android:text="Foot (ft)"

android:textAppearance="?android:attr/textAppearanceMedium" />

    <EditText
        android:id="@+id/editText2"
        android:layout_width="wrap_content"
        android:layout_height="wrap_content"
        android:layout_alignBaseline="@+id/textView2"
        android:layout_alignBottom="@+id/textView2"
        android:layout_marginLeft="30dp"
        android:layout_toRightOf="@+id/textView2"
        android:ems="10"
        android:inputType="numberDecimal"
        android:onClick="onClick" />

    <RadioGroup
        android:id="@+id/radioGroup2"
        android:layout_width="wrap_content"
        android:layout_height="wrap_content"
        android:layout_above="@+id/button1"
        android:layout_alignParentLeft="true"
        android:layout_alignRight="@+id/editText2"
        android:onClick="onClick"
        android:orientation="horizontal" >

        <RadioButton
            android:id="@+id/radioButton1"
            android:layout_width="wrap_content"
            android:layout_height="wrap_content"
            android:layout_gravity="left"
            android:checked="true"
            android:onClick="onClick"
            android:text="Length" />

        <RadioButton
            android:id="@+id/radioButton2"
            android:layout_width="wrap_content"
            android:layout_height="wrap_content"
            android:onClick="onClick"
            android:text="Weigth" />

        <RadioButton
            android:id="@+id/radioButton3"
            android:layout_width="wrap_content"
            android:layout_height="wrap_content"
            android:layout_gravity="right"
            android:onClick="onClick"
            android:text="Temp" />

    </RadioGroup>

    <Button
        android:id="@+id/button1"
        android:layout_width="wrap_content"
        android:layout_height="wrap_content"
        android:layout_alignParentBottom="true"
        android:layout_centerHorizontal="true"
        android:layout_marginBottom="79dp"
        android:onClick="onCalc"
        android:text="Convert" />

</RelativeLayout>
```

New functionality

```java
package com.ultinf.metricconverter;

import com.ultinf.metricconverter.R;

import android.app.Activity;
import android.os.Bundle;
import android.view.View;
import android.widget.EditText;
import android.widget.TextView;
import android.widget.Toast;

public class ConvertMetricActivity extends Activity {
        private EditText txtMetric;
        private EditText txtUSMetric;
        private TextView txLabel;
        private TextView txLabelUS;
        private int          iRadioBtn = 1;
        @Override
        protected void onCreate(Bundle savedInstanceState) {
                super.onCreate(savedInstanceState);
                setContentView(R.layout.activity_convert_metric);
                txLabel = (TextView) findViewById(R.id.textView1);
                txLabelUS = (TextView) findViewById(R.id.textView2);
                txtMetric =   (EditText)
findViewById(R.id.editText1);
                txtUSMetric = (EditText)
findViewById(R.id.editText2);
// Button btnCalculate = (Button) findViewById(R.id.button1);
        }

        // "OnClick property" of the text fields
        public void onClick(View view) {
                double inpVal, outVal;
                switch (view.getId()) {
                case R.id.editText1:
                        txtUSMetric.setText("");
                        break;

                case R.id.editText2:
                        txtMetric.setText("");
                        break;

                case R.id.radioButton1:
                        txLabel.setText("Meter (m)");
                        txLabelUS.setText("Foot (ft)");
                        iRadioBtn = 1;
                        clearFields();
                        break;

                case R.id.radioButton2:
```

```
                              txLabel.setText("Kilogram (kg)");
                              txLabelUS.setText("Pound (lb)");
                              iRadioBtn = 2;
                              clearFields();
                              break;

                 case R.id.radioButton3:
                              txLabel.setText("Celsius(C)");
                              txLabelUS.setText("Farenheit(F)");
                              iRadioBtn = 3;
                              clearFields();
                              break;

          }
      }

      private void clearFields()
      {
              txtUSMetric.setText("");
              txtMetric.setText("");
      }

      private double EUtoUS(double inpVal) {
              double outVal=0;
              switch (iRadioBtn) {
              case 1:
                      outVal = 3.281 * inpVal;
                      break;
              case 2:
                      outVal =  2.205 * inpVal;
                      break;
              case 3:
                      outVal =  (9*inpVal)/5 + 32;
                      break;
              }
              return outVal;
      }

      private double UStoEU(double inpVal) {
              double outVal=0;
              switch (iRadioBtn) {
              case 1:
                      outVal = 0.3048 * inpVal;
                      break;
              case 2:
                      outVal =  0.4536 * inpVal;
                      break;
              case 3:
                      outVal =  (inpVal-32)*5 / 9;
                      break;
              }
              return outVal;
      }
      public void onCalc(View view) {
```

```
                double inpVal, outVal;
                switch (view.getId()) {
                case R.id.button1:
                        if ( ((txtMetric.getText().length() == 0)
&&

        (txtUSMetric.getText().length() == 0)) ||

        ((txtMetric.getText().length() != 0) &&

(txtUSMetric.getText().length() != 0))
                                                )
                        {
                                Toast.makeText(this, "Please
enter a valid number in one of the fields ",

        Toast.LENGTH_LONG).show();
                                        clearFields();
                                        return;
                        }
                        if ( (txtMetric.getText().length() == 0) )
                        {
                                inpVal =
Double.parseDouble(txtUSMetric.getText().toString());
                                outVal = UStoEU(inpVal) ;

        txtMetric.setText(String.valueOf(outVal));
                        }
                        else
                        {
                                inpVal =
Double.parseDouble(txtMetric.getText().toString());
                                outVal = EUtoUS(inpVal);

        txtUSMetric.setText(String.valueOf(outVal));
                        }

                        break;
                }
        }

}
```

For a description of AndroidManifest.xml see The Manifest file.

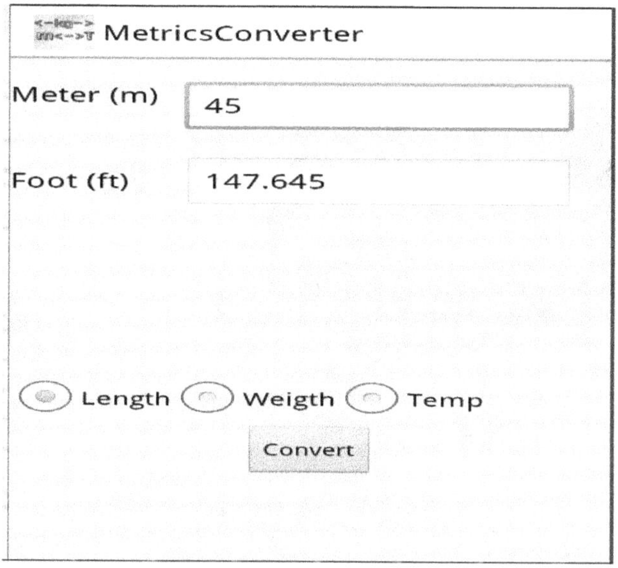

Figure 18: Metric Converter running

Part II: Basic Application Features

3. Application Fundamentals

Android applications are written in Java. The ADT tool compile Java code into an *.APK archive file (Android package). It contains all the contents of the application — executable code along with any data and resource files and it is the file that Android devices use to install the app.

During installation on a device, the Android operating system assigns to the app a unique ID (hidden from the app). The system sets permissions for that ID to access device data such as the SMS messages, user's contacts, the mountable storage (SD card), camera, Bluetooth, etc. Thus, only devices with ID assigned to that app can be accessed.

In this way, the Android system implements the principle of least privilege: each app has access only to the components that it requires to do its work and no more. This creates a very secure environment in which an app cannot access parts of the system for which it is not given permission.

Every app runs in its own Linux process (essentially an instance of Dalvik virtual machine) thus it is isolated from other apps.

Mobile devices are resource constrained, particularly in terms of RAM memory capacity. Consequently, a prime responsibility of the Android operating system is to ensure effective memory management of applications. It has the power to terminate processes in order to free up memory.

Android takes into consideration the process state when deciding whether that process should be terminated. It depends upon the status of the activities hosted by that process.

Thus, an application moves through a variety of states during its execution. An essential element of Android application development involves the ability of an application to respond to state change notifications from the operating system.

Let us take a closer look of the building blocks of an application.

Application Components

On Android, applications are like modules. Each application is made up of components in the form of activities and services which use data and exchange messages. They can be accessed by other applications. Thus, application developers do not need to rely on a specific set of APIs in order to achieve interoperability between their applications.

When the system starts a component, it starts the process for that app and instantiates the classes needed for the component. For example, if your app starts the activity in the music player app, that activity runs in the process that belongs to the music player app, not in your app's process. Therefore, unlike apps on most other systems, Android apps do not have a single entry point.

Android framework defines four main components: activity, service, broadcast receiver, and content provider. Each application does not need to use all of these components.

Activities

An activity represents a single screen with a user interface. An Android application can have several activities. For example, the app might have one activity that shows a list of new emails, another activity to compose an email, and another activity for attaching files to emails. Although the activities work together, each one is independent of the others. Moreover, a different app can start any one of these activities.

Services

A service is a component that runs in the background without providing a user interface. It performs time-consuming operations or remote processes tasks. It can communicate with other Android components and notify the user via intents. For example, a service might receive data over the network without blocking user interaction with an activity. Another component, such as an activity, can start the service in order to interact with it.

Content providers

A content provider manages the app data and shares it with other apps. Usually the application stores the data in the file system, a SQLite database or on the web. Through the content provider, other apps can query or even modify the data. For example, the Android system provides a content provider that manages the user's contact information or SMS messages. Any other app with the proper permissions can query the content provider to read and write information about a particular person.

Content providers may are also be used for updating data that is private to your app and not shared.

Broadcast receivers

A broadcast receiver is a component that make system-wide broadcast announcements. Many events originate from the Android system— e.g., announcing that the screen has turned off, the battery is low, etc. Apps can also send broadcasts messages — e.g., to let other apps know that some data has been captured and is available for them to use. More commonly broadcast receivers do not have a user interface; they are just a "gateway" to other components and are intended to do a minimal amount of work. However, they might initiate a service to perform some other work based on the event.

Because the system runs each app in a separate process with file permissions that restrict access to other apps, your app cannot directly activate a component from another app. The Android system, however, can activate a component in another app by using intents.

Intents are asynchronous messages which allow the application to request functionality from other Android components, e.g. from *services* or *activities*. Hereafter we describe them.

Intent

Three of the component types: activities, services, and broadcast receivers are activated by intents. Intents serve as messengers that request an action from other components.

The two most important pieces of an intent are the action and "data". Actions are constants, such as ACTION_VIEW (to bring up a viewer for the resource), ACTION_EDIT (to edit the resource), ACTION_PICK (to choose an available item given an Uri) or ACTION_SEND (to send the resource).

What Android refers to as "data" is an Uri, e.g. content://contacts/people representing a contact in the contacts database.

If the activity you intend to launch is one of your own, you may find it simplest to create an explicit intent, with parameter the component you wish to launch. For example, you could create an intent like this:

```
new Intent(this, MyActivity.class);
```

This would launch the MyActivity. It has be mentioned in your AndroidManifest.xml file, though not necessarily with any intent filter, since you are invoking it directly. Alternatively, you could put together an intent for some Uri, requesting a particular action:

```
Uri uri=Uri.parse("geo:"+lat.toString()+","+lon.toString());
Intent i=new Intent(Intent.ACTION_VIEW, uri);
```

Here, given that we have the latitude and longitude of some position (`lat` and `lon`, respectively) of type `Double`, we construct a geo scheme `Uri` and create an intent requesting to view this `Uri` with `ACTION_VIEW`. In some cases, you can start an activity to receive a result, in which case, the activity also returns the result in an Intent. See e.g. Exchanging data between activities

```
Intent in = new Intent();
...

startActivityForResult(in, 1);
...

// 4. Return data using the setData() method
    in.setData(Uri.parse("http://www.test.com"));

    setResult(RESULT_OK, in);
```

However, the real power of intents lies in the concept of *implicit* intents. It simply describes the type of action to perform (or the data). Then the system finds a component on the device that can perform the action and start it. If there are multiple components that can perform the action described by the intent, then the user selects which one to be used.

All Android components that have to be notified via intents must declare intent filters, so Android knows which intents should respond to that component. To do this, you need to add intent-filter elements to your AndroidManifest.xml file.

```
<intent-filter>
    <action android:name="android.intent.action.MAIN" />
    <category android:name="android.intent.category.LAUNCHER" />
</intent-filter>
```

E.g., if you have an email app with an activity for composing a new email, you can declare an intent filter to respond to "send" intents (in order to send a new email) like this:

```
<intent-filter>
        <action android:name="android.intent.action.SEND" />
        <data android:type="*/*" />
        <category android:name="android.intent.category.DEFAULT"
/>
    </intent-filter>
```

Then, if another app creates an intent with the ACTION_SEND action and pass it to startActivity(), the system may start your activity so the user can draft and send an email

For broadcast receivers, the intent simply defines the announcement being broadcast (for example, a broadcast to indicate the device battery is low includes only a known action string that indicates "battery is low").

The other component type, content provider, is not activated by intents. Rather, it is targeted by a request from a ContentResolver.

The Manifest File

One of the most important files of an application is its "manifest" file: AndroidManifest.xml. The Android system knows which components compose the application by reading this file, which must be at the root of the app project directory. It is generated automatically by New Android Project wizard and contains detailed information about the application collected through the wizard's dialogs:

```
<?xml version="1.0" encoding="utf-8"?>
```

```
<manifest
xmlns:android="http://schemas.android.com/apk/res/android"
    package="com.ultinf.metricconverter"
    android:versionCode="1"
    android:versionName="1.0" >

    <uses-sdk
        android:minSdkVersion="4"
        android:targetSdkVersion="19" />

    <application
        android:allowBackup="true"
        android:icon="@drawable/ic_launcher"
        android:label="@string/app_name"
        android:theme="@style/AppTheme" >
        <activity

android:name="com.ultinf.metricconverter.ConvertMetricActivity"
            android:label="@string/app_name" >
            <intent-filter>
                <action android:name="android.intent.action.MAIN"
/>

                <category
android:name="android.intent.category.LAUNCHER" />
            </intent-filter>
        </activity>
    </application>
</manifest>
```

Defining the minimal system requirements

Android is hosted on a variety of devices with different features and capabilities. It is important that all device and software requirements be properly defined in order to prevent your application from being installed on devices that lack the needed features. We could have the following defines in a manifest file:

- **minimum API Level**: android:minSdkVersion attribute of the <uses-sdk> element specifies the minimum version of the OS on which the application will run. For example, our app uses a minimum API introduced in Android 1.6 Donut (API level 4), that's why we declare these as requirements in our manifest file like this:

- `<uses-sdk android:minSdkVersion="4" android:targetSdkVersion="19" />`

- The other parameter defines target as API level 19 (Android 4.4 KitKat).

- **Specific devices or permissions:** Here we declare hardware and software features used or required by the app, such as a camera, Bluetooth services, or a multi-touch screen. Or we define any user permissions the app requires, such as Internet access or access to the user's contacts.

- The format is: `<uses-permission android:name="android.<device>"/>`

- and specifies that our application is going to use some `<device>`. For example in Available Sensors we define that we will use accelerometer in this way:

- `<uses-permission android:name="android.hardware.sensor.accelerometer"/>`

- Thus, devices that do not have an accelerometer and have an Android version lower than 1.6 cannot install our app.

- **version code of the application:** The format is:

- `<?xml version="<major>.<minor>" ?>` This value is used to identify the version number of your application. It can be used to programmatically determine whether an application needs to be upgraded. For example, in our case:

- `<?xml version="1.0" ?>` attribute specifies version = 1.

- **package name of the application:** E.g.:

  `package="com.ultinf.metricconverter"`

Defining the application components

One of the main goal of the manifest is to inform the system about the app's components and activities. The manifest file defines activity attributes within <application> element as follows:

- android:icon points to resources for application's icon
- android:name specifies the name of the application, which is a string defined in the strings.xml file.
- android:label specifies a string, which is a user-visible label for the app. In our case it is the same as the app's name
- android:theme specifies the theme of the app
- Inside the <application> element all app components have to be declared with following tags:
  - <activity> elements for activities
  - <service> elements for services
  - <receiver> elements for broadcast receivers
  - <provider> elements for content providers

Application components included in the source code but do not declared in the manifest are not visible to the system and, consequently, can never run.

The most important (and obligatory) tag is <activity>. Each app has at least one activity, which is defined in this tag together with the entry points of the application. ADT automatically creates it. Within the definition for this activity, there is an element named <intent-filter>:

- The action for the intent filter is named android.intent.action.MAIN to indicate that this activity serves as the entry point for the application.

- The category for the intent filter is named
  android.intent.category.LAUNCHER to indicate that the
  application can be launched from the device's Launcher icon.

Application Resources

An Android app consists from code plus resources such as images, audio files and XML configuration files related to the visual presentation of the app such as animations, menus, styles, colors, and the layout of activity user interfaces. The separation of the code from resources makes it easy to update various characteristics of the application without modifying code. Having sets of alternative resources gives possibility to optimize the app for a variety of device configurations, e.g. different screen sizes, resolutions, different languages, etc.

When ADT creates initially a new project, it creates a directory structure in the **project** folder, which except from source code keeps all the resources for that project. For example for our MetricConverter project, the following files and directories have been created:

```
Package Explorer Ⅹ
    MetricsConverter
        Android 4.4.2
            android.jar - D:\App\s\ADT_20140321\sdk\platforms\android-19
        Android Private Libraries
        Android Dependencies
            appcompat_v7.jar - D:\App\s\ADT_Projects\appcompat_v7\bin
        src
            com.ultinf.metricsconverter
                ConvertMetricsActivity.java
        gen [Generated Java Files]
            android.support.v7.appcompat
            com.ultinf.metricsconverter
                BuildConfig.java
                R.java
        assets
        bin
        libs
            android-support-v4.jar
        res
            drawable-hdpi
            drawable-ldpi
            drawable-mdpi
            drawable-xhdpi
            drawable-xxhdpi
            layout
                activity_convert_metrics.xml
            values
                strings.xml
                styles.xml
            values-v11
            values-v14
        AndroidManifest.xml
        ic_launcher-web.png
        lint.xml
```

- **Android 4.4.2**: Contains the .jar file of supporting API 19

- **Android Dependencies:** Contains the .jar file of downward compatible API 7

- **src:** The New Android Project wizard generate automatically application package in this directory. All the .java source files for our project are located in this subdirectory. In our example, there is only one file - ConvertMetricActivity.java, which is our main activity.

- **gen:** Contains automatically generated project files, such as the R class for resource index. Users are not expected to modify the content of this directory. The content of this directory is regenerated each time the project is compiled.

- **assets:** This directory contains all the assets used by our application, such as HTML, text files, databases, etc.
- **bin:** Contains the compiled class files and the installable Android package file for the project. In our case, this is MetricConverter.apk. Users are not expected to modify the content of this directory.
- **libs:** This directory contains all the class libraries needed for our application.
- **res:** Contains all the resources used in our application. ADT automatically generate the layout, string resources, and icons, image files, etc. Resources are organized in the following subfolders:
  - **color:** Contains color resources.
  - **drawable-<resolution>:** where <resolution> could be ldpi, mdpi, hdpi, xhdpi – contains all image files depending on the target screen resolutions. For each one the ADT defines a unique integer ID, which can be used to reference the resource from your app code or from other resources defined in XML. For example, if this folder contains an image file img1.jpg, the ADT generate a resource ID named R.drawable.img1.jpg, which you can use to reference the image and insert it in your user interface.
  - **layout:** Contains user interface resources. For example, our main layout activity_convert_metric.xml is placed here.
  - **values:** Contains various string resources and UI styles for different device configurations. For example, you can translate the strings into other languages and save those strings in separate files. Then, based on a language qualifier that you append to the resource directory's name (such as res/values-fr/ for French string values) and the user's language setting, the

Android system applies the appropriate language strings to your UI.

- o **values-v11** and **values-v14** correspond for API 11 and API 14 compliant devices.
- **Menu:** Contains menu resources, if any.

project.properties: This is a properties file that is used by the ADT while compiling and packaging the application.

Using ADT Editors

ADT provides a variety of editors to manipulate project files. In the following sections, we will use these editors to customize the project skeleton based on our project requirements.

Android Project Types

ADT provide GUIs and wizards to create all three types of projects - Android project, Library project, and Test project:

- An Android project contains all of the files and resources that are needed to build a project into an .apk file for installation.
- You can also designate an Android project as a library project, which allows it to be shared with other projects that depend on it. A library project cannot be installed onto a device. For more info, see Setting up a library project.
- Test projects include specific test functionality.

Android Lint

Android Lint tool scans Android application projects for potential bugs and most common mistakes. It also finds any inconsistencies in layouts, resources, and the manifest file. It is a powerful tool, which should be used during the development cycle in order to keep the application source code consistent. Select **Window** from main menu and check in **Run Android Lint** check box.

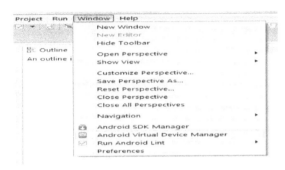

💻 *Figure 19: Lint*

4. Working with lists and tabs

Let us see how to put and select simple items from a list.

Selecting simple items from a list

The data for the list comes from an array of strings mStrings.

```
package com.ultunf.lsta;

import android.app.ListActivity;
import android.os.Bundle;
import android.view.View;
import android.widget.ArrayAdapter;
```

```
import android.widget.ListView;
import android.widget.Toast;

public class ListA extends ListActivity {
        private String[] mStrings =
                {
                        "Item 1", "Item 2", "Item 3", "Item 4"
                };
        private String txt;
        @Override
        public void onCreate(Bundle savedInstanceState) {
                super.onCreate(savedInstanceState);

                // The ListAdapter will map our array of strings
to TextViews
                setListAdapter(new ArrayAdapter<String>(this,

        android.R.layout.simple_list_item_1, mStrings));
                getListView().setTextFilterEnabled(true);
        }

        protected void onListItemClick(ListView l, View v, int
position, long id) {
                // TODO Auto-generated method stub
                super.onListItemClick(l, v, position, id);

                switch(position){

                case 0:
                        txt = "Selected: 1";
                        break;
                case 1:
                        txt = "Selected: 2";
                        break;
                case 2:
                        txt = "Selected: 3";
                        break;
                default:
                        txt = "Selected: default";
                        break;
                }

                Toast.makeText(getApplicationContext(), txt,
Toast.LENGTH_LONG).show();
        }
}
```

Later we will use this class to the following apps.

DEMO APP: Selecting Activities from Tabs

We are going to demonstrate the use of Tabs and Lists in a simplest way.

Because TabActivity was depreciated since API level 13, we will create a

project with `targetSdkVersion="10"`. Create new project
TabListA, with `package com.ultinf.tablista`. Select Empty
Activity check box with default name MainActivity.

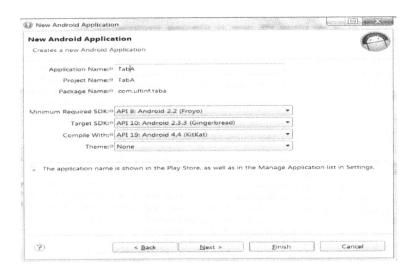

After ADT creates all the project files, you may also need to
change the compliance level of Java compiler to 1.6. (See
changing compliance).

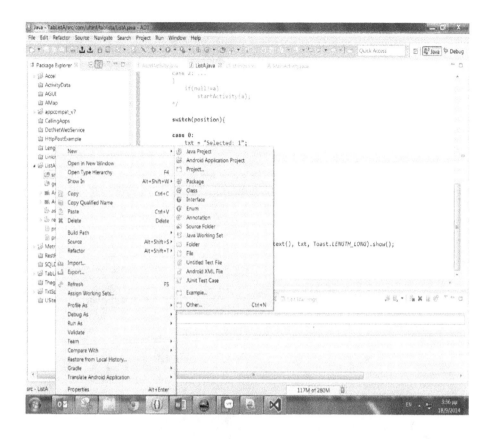

📓 *Figure 20: Selecting activities from tabs*

Replace it with the following code:

```java
package com.ultinf.tablista;

import android.app.TabActivity;
import android.content.Intent;
import android.os.Bundle;
import android.widget.TabHost;

@SuppressWarnings("deprecation")
public class MainActivity extends TabActivity {

    @Override
    protected void onCreate(Bundle savedInstanceState) {
        super.onCreate(savedInstanceState);

        final TabHost tabHost = getTabHost();
```

```
        tabHost.addTab(tabHost.newTabSpec("tab1")
                .setIndicator("list 1")
                .setContent(new Intent(this, List1.class)));
        tabHost.addTab(tabHost.newTabSpec("tab2")
                .setIndicator("numbers")
                .setContent(new Intent(this,
  TextSwitcher1.class)));

    }
}
```

Use an existing ListAdapter that will map an array of strings to TextViews

Add two layouts to Manifest.xml:

```
<activity android:name="com.ultinf.tablista.List1"/>
<activity android:name="com.ultinf.tablista.TextSwitcher1"/>
```

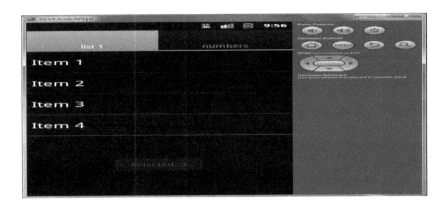

Figure 21: List Items

Selecting Activities from List

Here we present a List of Activities that start depending on which item in the list is clicked. The class extends ListActivity. The constructor creates a simple list in mStrings. OnCreate() method creates a setListAdapter()

which maps our array of strings to TextViews. We define
onListItemClick() listener that listen for a click event and reference the
position in the list. Then for each item clicked, we create a new Intent and
start corresponding Activity.

```
package com.ultunf.lsta;

import android.os.Bundle;
import android.app.ListActivity;
import android.content.Intent;
import android.view.View;
import android.widget.ArrayAdapter;
import android.widget.ListView;
import android.net.Uri;

public class LstActivity extends ListActivity {
        private String[] mStrings =
                {
                                "List", "Ultinf Web site", "SMS
Message", "E-Mail"
                };

        @Override
        public void onCreate(Bundle savedInstanceState) {
                super.onCreate(savedInstanceState);

                // A. The ListAdapter will map our array of
strings to TextViews
                setListAdapter(new ArrayAdapter<String>(this,

        android.R.layout.simple_list_item_1, mStrings));
                getListView().setTextFilterEnabled(true);
        }

        protected void onListItemClick(ListView l, View v, int
position, long id) {
                // TODO Auto-generated method stub
                super.onListItemClick(l, v, position, id);

                        Intent i;
                        switch(position){
                        case 0:
                                i = new Intent(this, ListA.class);
                                startActivity(i);
                                break;
                        case 1:
                                i = new
Intent(android.content.Intent.ACTION_VIEW);

                i.setData(Uri.parse("http://ultinf.com/"));
                                startActivity(i);
                                break;

                        case 2:
                                i = new
Intent(android.content.Intent.ACTION_SEND);
                                i.setType("text/plain");
```

```
                              i.putExtra(Intent.EXTRA_SUBJECT,
 "Subject of the message");   i.putExtra(Intent.EXTRA_TEXT, "This is
 a sample text");             startActivity(Intent.createChooser(i,
 "Apps that can respond to this"));
                              break;
              case 3:
                              i = new Intent(Intent.ACTION_SEND);
                              i.setData(Uri.parse("mailto:"));
                              String[] to = { "me1@example.com" ,
 "me2@example.com" };
                       String[] cc = { "me3@example.com" };
                       i.putExtra(Intent.EXTRA_EMAIL, to);
                       i.putExtra(Intent.EXTRA_CC, cc);
                       i.putExtra(Intent.EXTRA_SUBJECT, "Subject
 here...");
                       i.putExtra(Intent.EXTRA_TEXT, "Message here...");
                       i.setType("message/rfc822");
                       startActivity(Intent.createChooser(i, "Email"));
                              break;

              default:
                       i = new Intent("ListA");
              }

       }
 }
```

5. Application Issues

Changing compiler compliance level

Sometimes you need to target your app for low level e.g. API 10.

However changing simply `targetSdkVersion="10"` will result to a

compiler error:

```
Using 1.7 requires compiling with Android 4.4 (KitKat);
currently using API 10
```

The solution is to use previous Java compiler level. In order to change it,

right-click on Project's properties and select:

Java Compiler-> Enable project specific settings check box and

Use default compliance settings check box and from the right list view select level 1.6

Figure 22: Changing compliance settings

Adding app classes from API demos

Let's see step by step how a specific functionality can be added to our test project.

- Copy *.java Activity class to project/src , e.g. Intents.java.

```
import android.app.Activity;
import android.content.Intent;
import android.os.Bundle;
import android.view.View;
import android.view.View.OnClickListener;
import android.widget.Button;

public class Intents extends Activity {
    @Override
    protected void onCreate(Bundle savedInstanceState) {
        super.onCreate(savedInstanceState);

        setContentView(R.layout.intents);
    }

    public void onGetMusic(View view) {
        Intent intent = new Intent(Intent.ACTION_GET_CONTENT);
        intent.setType("audio/*");
        startActivity(Intent.createChooser(intent, "Select music"))
    }
```

Figure 23: Adding app classes

The setContentView(R.layout.intents); error prompts us that we have to add corresponding layout.

Copy Layout *.xml (intents.xml in our case) to res/layout.

We see several similar errors android:text="@string/intents"/> that prompt us to add string definitions.

- Add missing string definitions to res/values/string.xml:

```
<?xml version="1.0" encoding="utf-8"?>
<resources>
    <string name="app_name">AA4Tab</string>
    <string name="list1_name">List1_Tab</string>
    <string name="intents">Various Intents</string>
    <string name="get_music">Get Music</string>
    <string name="get_image">Get Image</string>
    <string name="get_stream">Get Stream</string>
</resources>
```

- Add new tab with Intents.class to AA4TabActivity.java

```
tabHost.addTab(tabHost.newTabSpec("tab6")
                          .setIndicator("intents")
                          .setContent(new Intent(this,
Intents.class)));
```

- Register Intents activity to Manifest.xml:

```
    <activity android:name="com.example.aa4tab.intents" >
    </activity>
```

- Run and test application.

Setting up a Library Project

A library project is a standard Android project, so you can create a new one in the same way as you would a new application project:

Select File > New > Project and let ADT create an ordinary project. On second window don't check Create custom launcher icon check box:

Set the other options as desired and click **Next**, follow the instructions to complete the wizard and create a new project. Then follow the steps below that could also be used to convert an existing application project into a library:

- In the Package Explorer, right-click the library project and select Properties.
- In the Properties window, select the Android properties group in the left pane and locate the Library properties in the right pane.
- Select **Library** check box and click **Apply**.
- Click **OK** to close the Properties window.

Figure 24: Making a project as an Android library

We can reference the library project in other Android application projects (see the Referencing a library project section). The most common case of a library project is appcompat v7 library. ADT provides automatic support for it.

Creating the manifest file

A library project's manifest file must declare all of the shared components that it includes, just as would a standard Android application. Usually it includes fewer sections. Especially for the case of appcompat_v7, it includes only min SDK version:

```
<?xml version="1.0" encoding="utf-8"?>
<manifest
xmlns:android="http://schemas.android.com/apk/res/android"
        package="android.support.v7.appcompat">
    <uses-sdk android:minSdkVersion="7"/>
        <application />
</manifest>
```

Adding Library .jar-AA

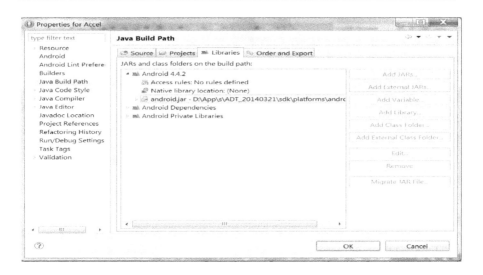

🖥 *Figure 25: Adding library references*

Referencing a library project

If you want to include to your app resources from a library project, make the following:

- In the Package Explorer, right-click the library project and select Properties.
- In the Properties window, select the Android properties group in the left pane and locate the Library properties in the right pane.

- Click Add to open the Project Selection dialog.
- From the list of available library projects, select a project and click OK then Apply.

- Click OK to close the Properties window.

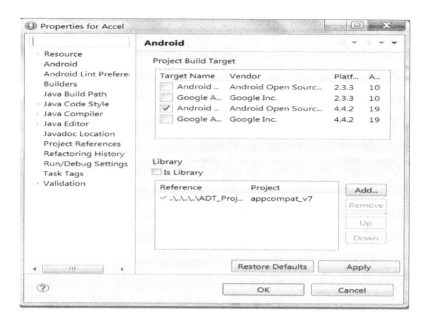

Figure 26: Adding a reference to a library project in the properties of an application project.

Automatic appcompat v7 library support

The support library does provide backward compatibility for numerous components of the Android SDK. One of the most common are Action Bar and Fragment API that appeared at API 11 (Android 3.0).

However, in most of our examples we target the older devices (but much bigger auditory) with minimum API 10 (Android 2.3.3 Gingerbread). Because our target SDK is set to 19, in which the Action Bar is on by default and our minimum supported SDK is set to 10, we need a support library. It is good practice to include the support library, because it provide backward-compatible versions. Android code templates tools included in Eclipse through the Android Development Tools (ADT) add it by default. Of course, it could be deselected, but it is not recommended.

With each new project, ATD creates additionally a new apcompat_v7_v<num> project, which is a little bit annoying. I keep only one apcompat_v7 project and re-direct each new project to that library by the following simple steps:

Re-direction of appcompat library

- Go to Library Panel by right-click on Project > Properties > Android
- Remove the new created apcompat_v7_v<num> library
- Press Add button and select existing apcompat_v7 library

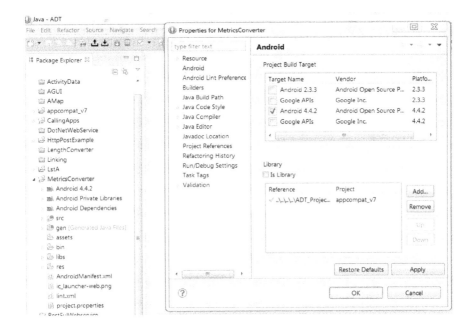

Figure 27: Re-direction of appcompat library

Refactor a project without appcompat_v7 :

Sometimes you need to use the capabilities of ADT of automatic creation of a project or use a ready-made project and later remove appcompat_7 support. Make the following:

- Right-click on Project > Properties > Android > Library. Remove appcompat placed in Reference. Select it and press Remove button.

- Delete **fragment_main.xml** and **Appcompat** file created in your Eclipse.

- Edit and change your **activity_main.xml** like the following:

```
<?xml version="1.0" encoding="utf-8"?>
<RelativeLayout
xmlns:android="http://schemas.android.com/apk/res/android"
    xmlns:tools="http://schemas.android.com/tools"
    android:layout_width="match_parent"
    android:layout_height="match_parent">

    <TextView
        android:layout_width="wrap_content"
        android:layout_height="wrap_content"
        android:text="@string/hello_world" />
</RelativeLayout>
```

- Change res/values/styles.xml:

```
<resources>
    <style name="AppBaseTheme"
parent="android:Theme.Light"></style>
    <!-- Application theme. -->
    <style name="AppTheme" parent="AppBaseTheme"> </style>
</resources>
```

- Change res/values-v11/styles.xml:

```
<resources>
```

```
    <style name="AppBaseTheme"
parent="android:Theme.Light"></style>
</resources>
```

- Change res/values-v14/styles.xml:

```
<resources>
    <style name="AppBaseTheme"
parent="android:Theme.Light"></style>
    <style name="AppTheme" parent="AppBaseTheme"></style>
</resources>
```

- Change **menu/main.xml** like this:

```
<menu xmlns:android="http://schemas.android.com/apk/res/android"
>
    <item
        android:id="@+id/action_settings"
        android:orderInCategory="100"
        android:title="@string/action_settings"/>
</menu>
```

- Finally change your **MainActivity.java** like the following:

```
import android.app.Activity;
import android.os.Bundle;

public class MainActivity extends Activity {

    @Override
    protected void onCreate(Bundle savedInstanceState) {
        super.onCreate(savedInstanceState);
        setContentView(R.layout.activity_main);}
}
```

After these steps, you have to clean the project in order a new R.java to be created. From top **Project** tab select **clean** option and your project is ready.

Problems with old SDK

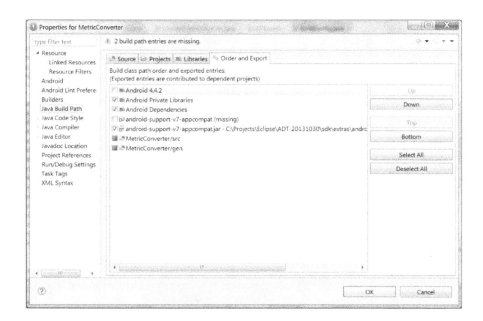

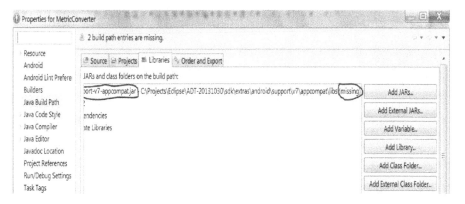

Adding a map to an application

The simplest way to add a map to an application is to specify it in the layout XML file for an activity. The following example layout file shows a Map Fragment instance added as the child of a RelativeLayout view:

```
<RelativeLayout
xmlns:android="http://schemas.android.com/apk/res/android"
```

```
        xmlns:tools="http://schemas.android.com/tools"
        android:layout_width="match_parent"
        android:layout_height="match_parent"
        tools:context=".AndroidTestActivity" >

    <fragment
                android:id="@+id/map"
                android:layout_width="match_parent"
                android:layout_height="match_parent"

    android:name="com.google.android.gms.maps.MapFragment"/>
    </RelativeLayout>
```

Assuming that the onCreate() method for the activity contains the standard code to load the layout resource file; the application should run and display a map:

```
@Override
protected void onCreate(Bundle savedInstanceState) {
        super.onCreate(savedInstanceState);
        setContentView(R.layout.activity_maps_demo);
}
```

In the event that a map is not displayed, check the following areas:

- If the application is running on an emulator, make sure that the emulator is running a version of Android that includes the Google APIs.

- Check the LogCat output for any areas relating to authentication problems with regard to the Google Maps API. This usually means the API key was entered incorrectly or that the application package name does not match that specified when the API key was generated.

- Verify that the correct entries and permissions have been added to the Manifest file, including all references to the package name and API key.

- Verify within the Google API Console that the Google Maps Android API has been enabled in the Services panel.

6. Android Apps with sensors and devices

See also:

http://developer.android.com/guide/topics/sensors/sensors_motion.html

DEMO APP: Accelerator Sensor

One of the most interesting features available on Android devices is **using Sensors**. Nowadays our smartphones are full of sensors and we can use them to do something useful in our app. This was not possible a couple of years ago when we were writing apps for PC desktops.

The most common mobile sensors are:

- Accelerator sensor
- GPS
- Proximity and rotation sensors
- Ligth sensor
- Temperature sensor
- Barometer sensor
- Magnetic sensor

Here we will explain how to obtain a list of sensors and how we can use one of them (**Accelerator sensor**, which is most possible to be available on any mobile device).

We want to create an app that shows the direction of moving the device from its current position. We just display the coordinates of the acceleration. Later this code can be used in various applications e.g. for games.

List of available sensors on our device

The first simple step is to list available sensors of our device.

Create a project named Accel with main activity AccelActivity. The ADT generates the skeleton project for us.

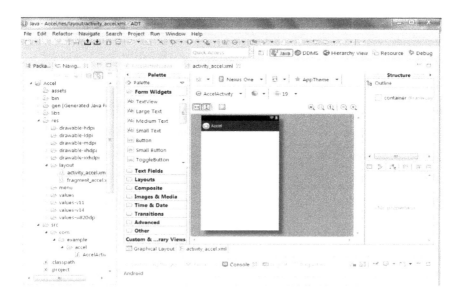

In Graphical Layout of activity_accel drag a 'TextView' form widget from Palette to white area.

Our activity_accel.xml is very simple:

```
<FrameLayout
xmlns:android="http://schemas.android.com/apk/res/android"
    xmlns:tools="http://schemas.android.com/tools"
    android:id="@+id/container"
    android:layout_width="match_parent"
    android:layout_height="match_parent"
```

```
tools:context="com.ultinf.accel.AccelActivity"
tools:ignore="MergeRootFrame" >

<TextView
    android:id="@+id/textView1"
    android:layout_width="294dp"
    android:layout_height="263dp"
    android:gravity="center"
    android:text="TView:"
    android:textSize="20sp" />
</FrameLayout>
```

If we need a specific sensor for our application, we have two different choices:

- Specify the sensor in the AndroidManifest.xml

E.g. <uses-permission android:name="android.hardware.sensor.accelerometer"/>

- Detect all the sensors in a list and check if the one we are interested on is available

If we specify it in the AndroidManifest.xml, we simply select **Permissions** tab and add to the name filed: **android.hardware.sensor.accelerometer**

Figure 28: Android Manifest Permissions

Alternatively, we may add explicitly to the AndroidManifest.xml file the following line: <uses-permission android:name="android.hardware.sensor.accelerometer".

This is our manifest file:

```xml
<?xml version="1.0" encoding="utf-8"?>
<manifest
xmlns:android="http://schemas.android.com/apk/res/android"
    package="com.example.accel"
    android:versionCode="1"
    android:versionName="1.0" >

    <uses-sdk
        android:minSdkVersion="8"
        android:targetSdkVersion="10" />

    <uses-permission
android:name="android.hardware.sensor.accelerometer"/>

    <application
        android:allowBackup="true"
        android:icon="@drawable/ic_launcher"
        android:label="@string/app_name"
        android:theme="@style/AppTheme" >
        <activity
            android:name="com.ultinf.accel.AccelActivity"
            android:label="@string/app_name" >
            <intent-filter>
                <action android:name="android.intent.action.MAIN"
/>

                <category
android:name="android.intent.category.LAUNCHER" />
            </intent-filter>
        </activity>
    </application>
</manifest>
```

In order to list all the sensor devices, just add to the main activity the following piece of code:

```java
package com.ultinf.accel;

import android.os.Bundle;

import java.util.List;
```

```
import com.example.accel.R;

import android.hardware.Sensor;
import android.hardware.SensorManager;
import android.widget.Toast;
import android.app.Activity;
import android.content.Context;

public class AccelActivity extends Activity {

        SensorManager sm;
        @Override

        protected void onCreate(Bundle savedInstanceState) {
                super.onCreate(savedInstanceState);
                setContentView(R.layout.activity_accel);

                // A. get sensor service

        sm=(SensorManager)this.getSystemService(Context.SENSOR_SE
RVICE);

                // B.  get the list of sensors
                List<Sensor> sensorList =
sm.getSensorList(Sensor.TYPE_ALL);

                String str = "Sensors: ";
                for (Sensor sensor: sensorList) {
                        str = str + sensor.getName() + " ";
                }

                Toast.makeText(getApplicationContext(), str,
Toast.LENGTH_LONG).show();

        }
}
```

At line A. we get the reference to the SensorManager, used to handle sensor, then at line B. we get the sensor list. Since we want to have all the sensors present in our smartphone, we use *Sensor.TYPE_ALL*. If we wanted just specific one, we can filter the list passing the type of the sensor we are looking for. For example, if we wanted to have all the accelerometer sensors, instead we could use:

List<Sensor> sensorList =

sm.getSensorList(Sensor.TYPE_ACCELEROMETER);

Once we have the list we can show it using a *ListView*, or simply print it with *Toast,* what we do in our case. When we run the program on smartphone device, it looks like the following:

📟 *Figure 29: List of sensors of a running device*

Once we have our sensors we may want to get information from them.

Sensor Events

In order to get information from a sensor we have select the sensor and register a listener for it. In our case, we are interesting on accelerator sensor so we have to add the listener:

```
//Register the sensor you are going to use and declare delay of
sensor
sm.registerListener(this,
sm.getDefaultSensor(Sensor.TYPE_ACCELEROMETER),
                    SensorManager.SENSOR_DELAY_GAME);
//SENSOR_DELAY_NORMAL
```

We register our listener and provide in the second parameter our sensor type (TYPE_ACCELEROMETER). Notice that the last parameter represents how fast we want to be notified when the value measured by the sensor changes. There are several values, e.g. SENSOR_DELAY_GAME is faster notification rate than SENSOR_DELAY_NORMAL. However, you should keep in mind that a too fast notification rate could have negative effects on your apps. E.g., the operation system could not handle on time all the events generated by the sensor.

To register a class as a listener we have to *implement* it as **SensorEventListener.** In our case, we do not create a new class, just add *implements* qualifier to our main Activity:

```java
public class AccelActivity extends Activity implements
SensorEventListener {
...
@Override
public void onAccuracyChanged(Sensor sensor, int accuracy)
    {
            // TODO Auto-generated method stub
    }
//This method is called when your mobile moves in any direction
@Override
public void onSensorChanged(SensorEvent event)
    { ...
    }
}
```

We need to implement explicitly two methods: onAccuracyChanged() and onSensorChanged(). The first one may be left empty, but it needs to be present. The other method is more interesting and it is called when the sensor detects some activity. In our case we simply display the x,y,z coordinates in a TextVIew.

```java
package com.ultinf.accel;
import android.os.Bundle;
import java.util.List;
import com.example.accel.R;
```

```
import android.hardware.Sensor;
import android.hardware.SensorManager;
import android.widget.Toast;
import android.app.Activity;
import android.content.Context;


import android.hardware.SensorEvent;
import android.hardware.SensorEventListener;
import android.widget.TextView;


public class AccelActivity extends Activity implements
SensorEventListener {
        float x,y,z;

        SensorManager sm;
        TextView tv;
        @Override
        protected void onCreate(Bundle savedInstanceState) {
                super.onCreate(savedInstanceState);
                setContentView(R.layout.activity_accel);
                tv=(TextView)findViewById(R.id.textView1);
                //get sensor service

        sm=(SensorManager)this.getSystemService(Context.SENSOR_SE
RVICE);

                //Register the sensor you are going to use and
declare delay of sensor

        sm.registerListener(this,sm.getDefaultSensor(Sensor.TYPE_
ACCELEROMETER),

        SensorManager.SENSOR_DELAY_GAME); //SENSOR_DELAY_NORMAL

                // Get the list of sensors
                List<Sensor> sensorList =
sm.getSensorList(Sensor.TYPE_ALL);

                String str = "Sensors: ";
                for (Sensor sensor: sensorList) {
                        str = str + sensor.getName() + " ";
                }

                Toast.makeText(getApplicationContext(), str,
Toast.LENGTH_LONG).show();
        }

        @Override
        public void onAccuracyChanged(Sensor sensor, int
accuracy)
        {
                // TODO Auto-generated method stub

        }
        //This method is called when your mobile moves in any
direction
        @Override
        public void onSensorChanged(SensorEvent event)
        {

        if(event.sensor.getType()==Sensor.TYPE_ACCELEROMETER)
                {
                        //get x, y, z values
```

```
                              float value[]=event.values;
                              x=value[0];
                              y=value[1];
                              z=value[2];

                              // Filter some directions
                              if( x > 2)
                              {
                                      String str = "x=" + x + ";
y=" + y + "; z=" + z;
                                      tv.setText(str);
                              }
                        }
                }
}
```

If we run the app, we see constantly changing of the coordinates:

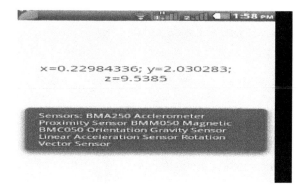

🖥 *Figure 30: Changing of the coordinates*

We can use this implementation to trigger some other event, when the smartphone is moved in some direction.

Simulate MotionEvent

In order to simulate display touch event we may add at the end of onSensorChanged() the following piece of code:

```
// Simulate MotionEvent
// Obtain MotionEvent object
        long downTime = SystemClock.uptimeMillis();
        long eventTime = SystemClock.uptimeMillis() + 100;
        float xm = 1.5f;
        float ym = 2.8f;
        int metaState = 0;
        MotionEvent motionEvent = MotionEvent.obtain(
                         downTime,
                         eventTime,
                         MotionEvent.ACTION_UP,
                         xm,
                         ym,
                         metaState
                );

        // Dispatch touch event to view
        this.dispatchTouchEvent(motionEvent);
```

Then every time when the sensor captures a motion event, it will produce another event: onTouch. Note that we set the parameter metaState to 0. A List of meta states can be found here:

http://developer.android.com/reference/android/view/KeyEvent.html#get MetaState()

This event could be captured with onTouchEvent() event handler and used to do some action. E.g., in a game app instead of touching the screen, we may keep or hands free and just move the smartphone, generating onTouch event.

In our case, we simply display a message:

```
@Override
public boolean onTouchEvent(MotionEvent event){

        if(event.getAction() == MotionEvent.ACTION_UP){

                String str = "On touch:: x=" + x + "; y=" + y +
"; z=" + z;
                Toast.makeText(getApplicationContext(), str,
Toast.LENGTH_LONG).show();
        }
        return super.onTouchEvent(event);
}
```

Text-To-Speech (TTS) device

One of the most useful features that Android provides is the text-to-speech synthesis, i.e. the capability of the device to "speak" text of different languages. This feature was introduced in version 1.6 of the Android platform. Here we will demonstrate TTS capabilities into our demo application.

DEMO APP: Text to Speak

Create a new project under the name TxtSpeak, with package `com.ultinf.txtspeak` and `TxtSpeakActivity`.

Before using the TTS engine it has to be properly been initialized. In order to get informed on whether this has happened, we implement an interface called OnInitListener. We do not use a separate class; just make our main activity implement `TextToSpeech.OnInitListener`. Here we construct the TextToSpeech object (**tts**).

```
package com.ultinf.txtspeak;

import android.os.Bundle;
import android.app.Activity;
import android.view.View;
import android.widget.Button;
import android.widget.EditText;

import java.util.Locale;
import com.ultinf.txtspeak.R;

import android.speech.tts.TextToSpeech;

public class TxtSpeakActivity extends Activity implements
TextToSpeech.OnInitListener{
        private TextToSpeech tts;
        private Button btn;
        private EditText txtSpeak;
        private EditText txtStatus;

        @Override
        public void onCreate(Bundle savedInstanceState) {
```

```
                super.onCreate(savedInstanceState);
                setContentView(R.layout.activity_txtspeak);

                tts=new TextToSpeech(this,this);
                btn=(Button)findViewById(R.id.button1);
                txtSpeak=(EditText)findViewById(R.id.editText1);

        txtStatus=(EditText)findViewById(R.id.editText2);


                btn.setOnClickListener(new
    View.OnClickListener() {
                        @Override
                        public void onClick(View v) {
                                speak();
                        }
                });
        }

        @Override
        public void onInit(int status) {
                if (status == TextToSpeech.SUCCESS) {
                        int result =
    tts.setLanguage(Locale.US);
                        if (result ==
    TextToSpeech.LANG_MISSING_DATA
                                                || result ==
    TextToSpeech.LANG_NOT_SUPPORTED) {
                                txtStatus.setText("Not
    supported language");
                        } else {
                                btn.setEnabled(true);
                                txtStatus.setText("TTS
    Succesful Initialization");
                                speak();
                        }
                } else {
                        txtStatus.setText("Initialization
    Failed");
                }
        }

        @Override
        protected void onDestroy() {
                if (tts != null) {
                        tts.stop();
                        tts.shutdown();}
                super.onDestroy();
        };

        private void speak() {
                String text = txtSpeak.getText().toString();
                tts.speak(text, TextToSpeech.QUEUE_FLUSH, null);
        }
}
```

Then on onCreate method, we initialize **tts**: tts=**new**

TextToSpeech(**this,this**); This is an asynchronous operation. The OnInit

(second argument **this**) will be invoked when the engine initialization has

completed with the accompanying status (it can be either
TextToSpeech.SUCCESS or TextToSpeech.ERROR). Then with
mTts.setLanguage(Locale.US) we set preferred language to US
English. Note that a language may not be available and the result will
indicate this with result. For example, the language may be available
for the locale but not for the specified country and variant. You may need
to install on your smartphone the voice data required for speech
synthesis. It could be done free from Google Play.

After initialization, we can use the TextToSpeech class to make the
device speak. The relevant method is named speak. It reads the text
written to text edit_txtSpeak. In onDestroy method we shut down
TextToSpeech engine.

Here is the layout file activity_txtspeak.xml :

```xml
<RelativeLayout
xmlns:android="http://schemas.android.com/apk/res/android"
    xmlns:tools="http://schemas.android.com/tools"
    android:layout_width="match_parent"
    android:layout_height="match_parent" >

    <EditText
        android:id="@+id/editText1"
        android:layout_width="wrap_content"
        android:layout_height="wrap_content"
        android:layout_alignParentLeft="true"
        android:layout_alignParentTop="true"
        android:layout_marginLeft="38dp"
        android:layout_marginTop="33dp"
        android:ems="10"
        android:text="Say Android" >

        <requestFocus />
    </EditText>

    <EditText
        android:id="@+id/editText2"
        android:layout_width="wrap_content"
        android:layout_height="wrap_content"
        android:layout_alignLeft="@+id/editText1"
        android:layout_alignParentBottom="true"
        android:layout_marginBottom="99dp"
        android:ems="10" />

    <Button
```

```
            android:id="@+id/button1"
            android:layout_width="wrap_content"
            android:layout_height="wrap_content"
            android:layout_alignLeft="@+id/editText1"
            android:layout_alignRight="@+id/editText1"
            android:layout_below="@+id/editText1"
            android:layout_marginLeft="35dp"
            android:layout_marginTop="84dp"
            android:text="CLICK" />
</RelativeLayout>
```

and the strings.xml:

```
<resources>

    <string name="app_name">TxtSpeak</string>
    <string name="title_activity_main">Text to Speak</string>

</resources>
```

We may use the manifest file that was built by default from ADT.

The ADT's emulator supports TTS with no configuration needed. The running application should look like the following:

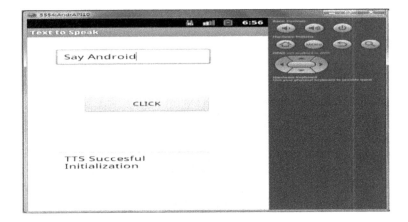

Figure 31: Text to speak engine

Apps can exchange data with Bluetooth devices

An Android device can wirelessly exchange data with other Bluetooth devices. The applications can use Bluetooth functionality through the Android Bluetooth APIs. The following functionality is available:

- Scan for other Bluetooth devices
- Manage multiple connections
- Queries for paired Bluetooth devices
- Establish RFCOMM channels
- Transfer data to and from other devices

7. Android SQLite database

Introduction

This chapter will cover the basics of SQLite use in the context of a working Android example.

SQLite is a very popular database and as the name suggests it is a "lite" version of a "full" SQL database like Oracle. It combines a subset of SQL queries with a very small memory requirements and good speed. Moreover, it is public domain and native for Android, so every Android application can use it.

We are going to demonstrate the basic features of SQLite via the following:

DEMO APP: SQLDbase

The interface of our application will look like the following:

📟 *Figure 32: SQL database running example*

We may add new elements with attributes "Name" and "Quantity", find or delete specific element giving its "Name". This this example will cover the basic operations with a database.

Create SQLDbase Project

Create a new Android Skeleton application with package name **com.aapp.sqldbase** and an activity called **SQLDbaseActivity.**

Database and Data Model

Creating the Database

The easiest way to create and open a database is to use a subclass of SQLiteOpenHelper. This class wraps up the logic of manipulating a database. Our class of SQLHelper will need to implement three methods:

- The constructor, chaining upward to the SQLiteOpenHelper:

```
public SQLHelper(Context context) {
                super(context, DATABASE_NAME, null,
DATABASE_VERSION); }
```

It provides the Context (e.g., of an Activity). Do not forget to include the super class.

- onCreate(), which passes a SQLiteDatabase object (db) that may be used to populate with tables and initial data. We will take a closer look at what this method is doing – in terms of execSQL() call after the snippet of code below.
- onUpgrade(), which passes a SQLiteDatabase object and the old and new version numbers, so you can include code to convert the database from the old schema to the new one. In the code below, we use the simplest approach to drop the old tables and create new ones.

Here is our SQLHelper class that, implements these three methods:

```
package com.aapp.sqldbase;
```

```
import android.content.ContentValues;
import android.content.Context;
import android.database.Cursor;
import android.database.sqlite.SQLiteDatabase;
import android.database.sqlite.SQLiteOpenHelper;

public class SQLHelper extends SQLiteOpenHelper {
        public static final String COL_ID = "_id";
        public static final String COL_ITEMNAME = "itemname";
        public static final String COL_QUANTITY = "quantity";

        private static final int DATABASE_VERSION = 1;
        private static final String DATABASE_NAME = "item.db";
        private static final String TABLE_ITEMS = "items";

        public SQLHelper(Context context) {
                super(context, DATABASE_NAME, null,
DATABASE_VERSION);
        }

        @Override
        public void onCreate(SQLiteDatabase db) {
                String CREATE_ITEMS_TABLE = "CREATE TABLE " +
                TABLE_ITEMS + "("
                + COL_ID + " INTEGER PRIMARY KEY," +
COL_ITEMNAME
                + " TEXT," + COL_QUANTITY + " INTEGER" +
")";
                db.execSQL(CREATE_ITEMS_TABLE);
        }

        @Override
        public void onUpgrade(SQLiteDatabase db, int oldVersion,
int newVersion)      {
                db.execSQL("DROP TABLE IF EXISTS " + TABLE_ITEMS);
                onCreate(db);
        }

        public void addItem(Item item) {

        ContentValues values = new ContentValues();
        values.put(COL_ITEMNAME, item.getItemName());
        values.put(COL_QUANTITY, item.getQuantity());

        SQLiteDatabase db = this.getWritableDatabase();

        db.insert(TABLE_ITEMS, null, values);
        db.close();
}


        public boolean deleteItem(String itemname) {

                boolean result = false;

                String query = "Select * FROM " + TABLE_ITEMS +
" WHERE " + COL_ITEMNAME + " = " + "\"" + itemname + "\"";

                SQLiteDatabase db = this.getWritableDatabase();

                Cursor cursor = db.rawQuery(query, null);

                Item item = new Item();
```

```
                    if (cursor.moveToFirst()) {

            item.setID(Integer.parseInt(cursor.getString(0)));
                        db.delete(TABLE_ITEMS, COL_ID + " =
?",
                        new String[] {
        String.valueOf(item.getID()) });
                        cursor.close();
                        result = true;
                }
            db.close();
                return result;
        }

        public Item findItem(String itemname) {
                String query = "Select * FROM " + TABLE_ITEMS +
  " WHERE " + COL_ITEMNAME + " = \"" + itemname + "\"";

                SQLiteDatabase db = this.getWritableDatabase();

                Cursor cursor = db.rawQuery(query, null);

                Item item = new Item();

                if (cursor.moveToFirst()) {
                        cursor.moveToFirst();

            item.setID(Integer.parseInt(cursor.getString(0)));
                        item.setItemName(cursor.getString(1));

            item.setQuantity(Integer.parseInt(cursor.getString(2)));
                        cursor.close();
                } else {
                        item = null;
                }
            db.close();
                return item;
        }
}
```

This class is added to the project by right clicking on the project and selecting New>Class from context menu.

Then provide Name: SQLHelper and click "Finish". Next, copy the code above and replace it to the default generated code.

In the same way, you may add the two other classes provided later in this chapter.

For creating tables and indexes, we need to call execSQL() on our onCreate() method.

```
public void onCreate(SQLiteDatabase db) {
        String CREATE_ITEMS_TABLE = "CREATE TABLE " + TABLE_ITEMS
+ "("
            + COL_ID + " INTEGER PRIMARY KEY," + COL_ITEMNAME
            + " TEXT," + COL_QUANTITY + " INTEGER" + ")";
        db.execSQL(CREATE_ITEMS_TABLE);
}
```

This will create a table TABLE_ITEMS = "items", with a primary key column COL_ID = "_id" that is an auto-incremented integer (i.e., SQLite will assign the value for you when you insert rows), with two data columns: COL_ITEMNAME = "itemname" (string). and COL_QUANTITY = "quantity" (integer). SQLite will automatically create an index for primary key column. You could add other indexes here via some CREATE INDEX statements.

Database operations

Having a database and one or more tables, we would like to put some data in them. This can be done in two ways. We can always use execSQL(), just like we did for creating the table. The execSQL() method can handle any general SQL statement with INSERT, UPDATE, DELETE etc.

The alternative is to use the insert(), update(), and delete() methods of the SQLiteDatabase object, which eliminate much of the SQL syntax and is simpler. We will use the second approach.

Insert   The insert() method takes the name of the table, the name of one column (here is **null**), and a ContentValues with the values we want to put into the row. The **null**

---

parameter is for the case where the ContentValues instance is empty –
then NULL value will be assigned to the column. For example, we
insert() a new row into our Items table:

```java
public void addItem(Item item) {

    ContentValues values = new ContentValues();
    values.put(COL_ITEMNAME, item.getItemName());
    values.put(COL_QUANTITY, item.getQuantity());

    SQLiteDatabase db = this.getWritableDatabase();

    db.insert(TABLE_ITEMS, null, values);
    db.close();
}
```

Delete   The delete() method takes the name of the table,
with optional WHERE clause, and the corresponding
parameters to fill into it. For example, here we delete() a row from our
Items table, given its ID (item.getID()):

```java
db.delete(TABLE_ITEMS, COL_ID + " = ?",
          new String[] { String.valueOf(item.getID()) });
```

Queries   As with previous methods, we have two main
options for retrieving data from a SQLite database
using:

- rawQuery() to invoke a SELECT statement directly, or
- query() to build up a query from its component parts. (Not be
  covered here)

The simplest solution is to use rawQuery(). It called with an SQL SELECT statement as parameter. The SELECT statement can include positional parameters as a second parameter (null in our case):

```
String query = "Select * FROM " + TABLE_ITEMS + " WHERE " +
COL_ITEMNAME + " = \"" + itemname + "\"";

SQLiteDatabase db = this.getWritableDatabase();

Cursor cursor = db.rawQuery(query, null);
```

The return value is a Cursor, which contains methods for iterating over results (see below).

However, using raw queries could become complicated if some parts of the query are dynamic, e.g.

when the set of columns you need to retrieve is not known at compile time. In this case the other method - query() should be used. (Not covered here).

Using Cursors   No matter what kind of query method is used, you get a Cursor back. This is a concept used in many database systems. With the cursor, you can:

- Iterate over the rows via moveToFirst(), moveToNext(), and isAfterLast() having the number of rows via getCount()
- Find out the names of the columns via getColumnNames()
- Convert them into column numbers via getColumnIndex(), and get values for the current row for a given column via methods like getString(), getInt(), etc.
- Convert them into column numbers via getColumnIndex(), and get values for the current row for a given column via methods like getString(), getInt(), etc.

- At the end we should release the cursor's resources via close()

For example, we iterate over Items table entries:

```
Cursor cursor = db.rawQuery(query, null);
              Item item = new Item();
              if (cursor.moveToFirst()) {
                      cursor.moveToFirst();
         item.setID(Integer.parseInt(cursor.getString(0)));
                      item.setItemName(cursor.getString(1));
         item.setQuantity(Integer.parseInt(cursor.getString(2)));
                      cursor.close();
              } else {
                      item = null;
              }
```

Database Model

Create the Item class. This class is our model and contains the data we will save in the database and show and retrieve in our interface. Check getters and setters section to see how to generate automatically this class:

```
package com.aapp.sqldbase;

public class Item {
        private int id;
        private String itemname;
        private int quantity;

        public Item() {}

        public Item(int id, String itemname, int quantity) {
                this.id = id;
                this.itemname = itemname;
                this.quantity = quantity;
        }
```

```
        public Item(String itemname, int quantity) {
                this.itemname = itemname;
                this.quantity = quantity;
        }

        public void setID(int id) {
                this.id = id;
        }

        public int getID() {
                return id;
        }

        public void setItemName(String itemname) {
                this.itemname = itemname;
        }

        public String getItemName() {
                return itemname;
        }

        public void setQuantity(int quantity) {
                this.quantity = quantity;
        }

        public int getQuantity() {
                return quantity;
        }
}
```

User Interface

Change your *activity_database.xml* layout file in
the *res/layout* folder to the following. This layout has three
buttons for adding, deleting and searching items:

```
<LinearLayout
xmlns:android="http://schemas.android.com/apk/res/android"
    xmlns:tools="http://schemas.android.com/tools"
    android:id="@+id/LinearLayout1"
    android:layout_width="match_parent"
    android:layout_height="match_parent"
    android:orientation="vertical"
    tools:context=".SQLDbaseActivity" >

    <TableLayout
        android:layout_width="match_parent"
```

```
            android:layout_height="wrap_content" >

        <TableRow
            android:id="@+id/tableRow1"
            android:layout_width="wrap_content"
            android:layout_height="wrap_content" >

            <TextView
                android:id="@+id/textView1"
                android:layout_width="wrap_content"
                android:layout_height="wrap_content"
                android:text="Item ID:"
android:textAppearance="?android:attr/textAppearanceLarge" />

            <TextView
                android:id="@+id/itemID"
                android:layout_width="wrap_content"
                android:layout_height="wrap_content"
                android:text="Not assigned"
android:textAppearance="?android:attr/textAppearanceLarge" />

        </TableRow>

        <TableRow
            android:id="@+id/tableRow2"
            android:layout_width="wrap_content"
            android:layout_height="wrap_content" >

            <TextView
                android:id="@+id/textView2"
                android:layout_width="wrap_content"
                android:layout_height="wrap_content"
                android:text="Name"
android:textAppearance="?android:attr/textAppearanceLarge" />

            <EditText
                android:id="@+id/itemName"
                android:layout_width="wrap_content"
                android:layout_height="wrap_content"
                android:ems="10" >

                <requestFocus />
            </EditText>

        </TableRow>

        <TableRow
            android:id="@+id/tableRow3"
            android:layout_width="wrap_content"
            android:layout_height="wrap_content" >

            <TextView
                android:id="@+id/textView3"
                android:layout_width="wrap_content"
                android:layout_height="wrap_content"
                android:text="Quantity"
android:textAppearance="?android:attr/textAppearanceLarge" />

            <EditText
                android:id="@+id/itemQuantity"
```

```xml
                        android:layout_width="wrap_content"
                        android:layout_height="wrap_content"
                        android:ems="10" />

            </TableRow>
        </TableLayout>

        <LinearLayout
            android:layout_width="match_parent"
            android:layout_height="wrap_content"
            android:gravity="center_horizontal" >

            <Button
                android:id="@+id/button1"
                android:layout_width="wrap_content"
                android:layout_height="wrap_content"
                android:onClick="newItem"
                android:text="@string/add_string" />

            <Button
                android:id="@+id/button2"
                android:layout_width="wrap_content"
                android:layout_height="wrap_content"
                android:onClick="lookupItem"
                android:text="@string/find_text" />

            <Button
                android:id="@+id/button3"
                android:layout_width="wrap_content"
                android:layout_height="wrap_content"
                android:onClick="removeItem"
                android:text="@string/delete_text" />

        </LinearLayout>
</LinearLayout>
```

Change your SQLDbaseActivity class to the following:

```java
package com.aapp.sqldbase;

import com.example.database.R;

import android.os.Bundle;
import android.app.Activity;
import android.view.Menu;
import android.view.View;
import android.widget.EditText;
import android.widget.TextView;


public class SQLDbaseActivity extends Activity {

        TextView idView;
        EditText productBox;
        EditText quantityBox;

        @Override
        protected void onCreate(Bundle savedInstanceState) {
                super.onCreate(savedInstanceState);
                setContentView(R.layout.activity_database);
```

```
        idView = (TextView) findViewById(R.id.itemID);
        productBox = (EditText) findViewById(R.id.itemName);
        quantityBox = (EditText) findViewById(R.id.itemQuantity);
        }

        @Override
        public boolean onCreateOptionsMenu(Menu menu) {
                return true;
        }

    public void newItem (View view) {
        SQLHelper dbHandler = new SQLHelper(this);

        int quantity =
            Integer.parseInt(quantityBox.getText().toString());

        Item item =
            new Item(productBox.getText().toString(),
quantity);

        dbHandler.addItem(item);
        productBox.setText("");
        quantityBox.setText("");
    }

    public void lookupItem (View view) {
        SQLHelper dbHandler = new SQLHelper(this);

        Item item =
dbHandler.findItem(productBox.getText().toString());

        if (item != null) {
                idView.setText(String.valueOf(item.getID()));

quantityBox.setText(String.valueOf(item.getQuantity()));
        } else {
                idView.setText("Nothing Found!");
        }
    }

    public void removeItem (View view) {
        SQLHelper dbHandler = new SQLHelper(this);

        boolean result = dbHandler.deleteItem(
            productBox.getText().toString());

        if (result)
            {
                        idView.setText("Record Deleted");
                        productBox.setText("");
                        quantityBox.setText("");
            }
              else
                    idView.setText("No Match Found");
            }
}
```

Change res/values/strings.xml to the following:

```
<?xml version="1.0" encoding="utf-8"?>
<resources>
    <string name="app_name">SQLDbase</string>
    <string name="action_settings">Settings</string>
    <string name="itemID">Item ID</string>
    <string name="add_string">Add</string>
    <string name="find_text">Find</string>
    <string name="delete_text">Delete</string>
</resources>
```

Here is AndroidManifest.xml:

```
<?xml version="1.0" encoding="utf-8"?>
<manifest
xmlns:android="http://schemas.android.com/apk/res/android"
    package="com.example.database"
    android:versionCode="1"
    android:versionName="1.0" >

    <uses-sdk
        android:minSdkVersion="8"
        android:targetSdkVersion="19" />

    <application
        android:allowBackup="true"
        android:icon="@drawable/ic_launcher"
        android:label="@string/app_name"
        android:theme="@style/AppTheme" >
        <activity
            android:name="com.aapp.sqldbase.SQLDbaseActivity"
            android:label="@string/app_name" >
            <intent-filter>
                <action android:name="android.intent.action.MAIN"
/>

                <category
android:name="android.intent.category.LAUNCHER" />
            </intent-filter>
        </activity>
    </application>

</manifest>
```

Running the application

Install your application and use Add, Search and Delete buttons.

Restart the application to validate that the data is still there.

8. Communication with Internet HTTP Server

If you own a web site, you may find useful the possibility to provide your app with data from it. In this way the Android app does not change, but may display different data. If you write a good app you may attract more users to launch it often my make it dynamic: you may provide it with various data from your web site that could be changed regularly: PUSH messages, daily news, fetch content from data sources from the web, have a frequently updated quiz, etc.

Here we describe the first simple step of communication with HTTP server: a basic app that opens a HTTP connection and sends through it to the server encrypted user name and password. On the remote side, the server decrypts those and sends back to the app a reply. Later in the next sub-chapter, we will describe more powerful approach, by using JSON objects.

DEMO APP: HTTPComm

The running app should look like the following:

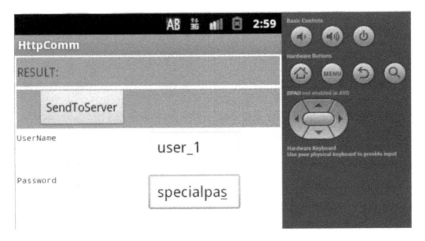

📷 *Figure 33: Http Comm running app*

Create a project named HTTPComm with main activity HTTPComm Activity and activity_http_comm layout. The ADT generates the skeleton project for us.

Normally, first we describe GUI, which gives us a feeling of the app and later the main activity. However, here we want to emphasize on HTTP communication that is why we switch the order.

The main activity HttpComm **extends** Activity class. Since we have to catch OnClick event we may have used instead: HttpComm **extends** Activity `implements OnClickListener{}`.However, since we have only one button click event, we provide here alternative online definition:

```
sendToServ.setOnClickListener(new Button.OnClickListener(){
                    public void onClick(View v)
                    {
                            try
                            {
                                    GetText();
                            }
                            catch(Exception ex)
                            {
                                    status.setText("url
ecxeption!");
```

```
                                        }
                            }
            });
```

Clicking on SendToServer button triggers the GetText procedure.

```java
package com.ultinf.httpcomm;

import java.io.BufferedReader;
import java.io.InputStreamReader;
import java.io.OutputStreamWriter;
import java.io.UnsupportedEncodingException;
import java.net.URL;
import java.net.URLConnection;
import java.net.URLEncoder;
import android.app.Activity;
import android.os.Bundle;
import android.view.View;
import android.widget.Button;
import android.widget.EditText;
import android.widget.TextView;

public class HttpComm extends Activity {

        TextView status;
        EditText username,password;
        String UserName,Passwd;

        @Override
        public void onCreate(Bundle savedInstanceState) {
                super.onCreate(savedInstanceState);
                setContentView(R.layout.activity_http_comm);

                status  = (TextView)findViewById(R.id.output);
                username=(EditText)findViewById(R.id.name);
                password
        =(EditText)findViewById(R.id.password);

                Button
sendToServ=(Button)findViewById(R.id.save);

                // A. Inline setOnClickListener definition
                        sendToServ.setOnClickListener(new
Button.OnClickListener(){
                        public void onClick(View v)
                        {
                                try
                                {
                                        GetText();
                                }
                                catch(Exception ex)
                                {
                                        status.setText("url
ecxeption!");
                                }
                        }
                });
```

```java
        }

        public void GetText() throws UnsupportedEncodingException
        {
                UserName = username.getText().toString();
                Passwd              =
password.getText().toString();

                status.setText("Before sending ...");

                // A1. Preparing and encoding name-value pairs:
                String data = URLEncoder.encode("name", "UTF-8")
+ "=" + URLEncoder.encode(UserName, "UTF-8");
                data += "&" + URLEncoder.encode("pass", "UTF-8")
+ "=" + URLEncoder.encode(Passwd, "UTF-8");

                String txtResponse = "";
                BufferedReader rd=null;

                try
                {
                        URL url = new
URL("http://bitinf.com/httpinf//httppost.php");

                        URLConnection conn =
url.openConnection();
                        conn.setDoOutput(true);
                        // B. Send data
                        OutputStreamWriter wr = new
OutputStreamWriter(conn.getOutputStream());
                        wr.write(data);
                        wr.flush();

                        //C. Receive the response
                        rd = new BufferedReader(new
InputStreamReader(conn.getInputStream()));
                        String line = null;

                        while((line = rd.readLine()) != null)
                        {
                                txtResponse += line + "\n";
                        }

                }
                catch(Exception ex)
                {
                        status.setText("Connection Error!");
                }

                // Close connection
                try
                {
                        rd.close();
                }
                catch(Exception ex)
                {
                        status.setText("Closing connection
Error!");
                }

                status.setText(txtResponse);
        }
```

```
}
```

From remote side, the server receives the post request, does decode ($_POST['name']) and $_POST['pass']) and simply display the values:

Here is the .php script that does the job:

```php
<?php
    $name   = urldecode($_POST['name']);
    $pass   = urldecode($_POST['pass']);

    print " ==== POST DATA Reply  ====>
UserName: $name
Pass    : $pass
        Successful Reply from HTTP Server "
?>
```

The GUI is designed in activity_http_coms.xml layout in Graphical Layout in the following manner:

Select Table Layout, add Table Row with two TextView.

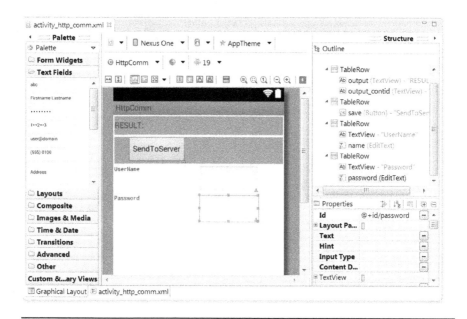

💻 *Figure 34: Http Comm Graphical Layout*

Alternatively, just replace the content of activity_http_coms.xml with the following code:

```
<TableLayout
 xmlns:android="http://schemas.android.com/apk/res/android"
  android:layout_width="wrap_content"
    android:layout_height="wrap_content"
        android:stretchColumns="*" android:background="#ffffff">


        <TableRow android:background="#969BB8"
android:layout_margin="2dip">

            <TextView
                android:id="@+id/output"
                android:layout_width="wrap_content"
                android:layout_height="wrap_content"
                android:padding="1px"
                android:text="@string/output_label" />

                <TextView
                    android:id="@+id/output_contid"
                    android:layout_width="fill_parent"
                    android:layout_height="wrap_content"
                    android:padding="8dp"
                    android:text="@string/output_cont" />

        </TableRow>

        <TableRow
            android:layout_width="match_parent"
            android:layout_margin="2dip"
            android:background="#969BB8" >

        <Button
            android:id="@+id/save"
            android:layout_width="wrap_content"
            android:layout_gravity="center"
            android:text="SendToServer" />

        </TableRow>

      <TableRow android:background="#ffffff"
android:layout_margin="2dip">

          <TextView
              style="@style/CodeFont"
              android:layout_width="5dip"
              android:layout_gravity="left"
              android:text="@string/UserName" />

          <EditText
              android:id="@+id/name"
              android:layout_width="wrap_content"
              android:layout_gravity="left"
              android:gravity="left"
              android:width="110dp" />
```

```
            </TableRow>

            <TableRow android:background="#ffffff"
    android:layout_margin="2dip">

                <TextView style="@style/CodeFont"
                    android:text="@string/Password"
    android:layout_gravity="left"/>

                <EditText
                        android:id="@+id/password"
                        android:layout_width="wrap_content"
                        android:layout_gravity="left"
                        android:width="110dp" />
            </TableRow>
    </TableLayout>
```

📖 Note: When using existing projects, always check that the API
version of the project correspond to the API version of the
Graphical Layout (see Graphical Layout with screenshot of this
project).

Do not for get to add to Manifest file the following permission:

```
    <uses-permission
    android:name="android.permission.INTERNET"></uses-permission>
```

JSON Objects

For a description of JSON objects see < What is JSON? > In short, a
JSON object is a list of key-value pairs or JSON objects. This is a very
useful format to organize, store and exchange data between websites
and mobile devices.

Here is a simple example of a JSON object:

```
{
"name" : "Lyza",
```

```
"id" : 1517,
"pass" : "secretpass",
"picture: "Lyza.bmp",
}
```

We may create JSON object and fill it up with data by using JSONObject class. The above JSON object is created and initialized by the following snippet of code:

```
        public void createJSON() {
                imageview
 =(ImageView)findViewById(R.id. imageView1);

                jsonObj = new JSONObject();
                try {
                        jsonObj.put("name", "Lyza");
                        jsonObj.put("id", 1517);
                        jsonObj.put("pass", "secretpass");
                        jsonObj.put("picture", imageview );
                } catch (JSONException e) {
                        e.printStackTrace();
                }
        }
```

Nowadays many popular websites (Facebook, Twitter, YouTube, Flickr, etc.) provide APIs to their users, allowing them to retrieve content in JSON format. That content can be lists of "likes" about an article, pictures, songs or video clips, etc. Those JSON APIs allow retrieving all those information dynamically. Usually, you have to register in their developer section, in order to obtain an API key. Then, you have to read the documentation on such sites in order to understand how each API work.

If you have your own website, you can provide a web page that returns JSON content. That page will be called by the application whenever needed to fill the screen content.

In the following snippet of code we implement ReceiveJSON class as an extension of AsyncTask.

```java
class ReceiveJSON extends AsyncTask<String, String, String>{
        ProgressDialog dialog;
        String JSON_URL = "http://bitinf.com/httpinf/Json.php";
        outpTxt = (TextView)findViewById(R.id.outpTxt);

        @Override
        protected void onPreExecute() {
                super.onPreExecute();
                status.setText("onPreExecute()");
                dialog = new ProgressDialog(HttpComm.this);
                dialog.setMessage("Loading, please wait");
                dialog.setTitle("Connecting to JSON server");
                dialog.show();
                dialog.setCancelable(false);
        }

        @Override
        protected String doInBackground(String...) {
        String receiveString = null;
        HttpResponse httpResponse;
        StatusLine statusLine;
        try {
                HttpClient httpClient = new DefaultHttpClient();
                httpResponse = httpClient.execute(new
HttpGet(JSON_URL));
                statusLine = httpResponse.getStatusLine();
                        if(statusLine.getStatusCode() ==
HttpStatus.SC_OK){
        ByteArrayOutputStream bytOut = new
ByteArrayOutputStream();

        httpResponse.getEntity().writeTo(bytOut);
        bytOut.close();
        receiveString = bytOut.toString();

        outpTxt.setText(receiveString);

                } else{
                                        // Close the connection.
        outpTxt.setText("try Exception");

        httpResponse.getEntity().getContent().close();
        throw new IOException(statusLine.getReasonPhrase());
                }
                } catch (ClientProtocolException e) {

        outpTxt.setText("ClientProtocolException");
                } catch (IOException e) {
                        outpTxt.setText("IOException");
                }
                return receiveString;
        }

        @Override
        protected void onPostExecute(String result) {
                super.onPostExecute(result);
```

```
                    outpTxt.setText("After onPost");
        }
}
```

Three major functions have to be defined: onPreExecute(),
doInBackground() and onPostExecute().

onPreExecute() creates a progress dialog while asynchronously in
doInBackground() an httpClient attempts to connect to the web page
with JSON_URL. If the connection is successful it gets the JSON object
by httpResponse = httpClient.execute(**new** HttpGet(JSON_URL)); which
is consequently converted to a ByteArrayOutputStream by
httpResponse.getEntity().writeTo(bytOut); At this point we may use the
information of bytOut. In a simple case as our, we just convert it as a
string and display it on a text view outpTxt.

When we execute the code, we receive from web site the JSON
object described in What is JSON?

PART III:
Tips & Tricks

Make a good looking and efficient application

Here are some simple but efficient tips to help you make a good application,

- A good mobile application must be **fast**, and **stable**.
- Avoid too **large** pictures. Do not add **too many** pictures on your screens: if necessary, **split** your screen into multiple screens.
- Make sure your application looks well on various screen **sizes** and **orientations**. Use pixel sizes instead of percentages.
- Use **custom fonts** and different **font styles** of your application texts. Use both large and small text sizes on the same screen. Here are some websites providing free fonts: http://www.1001freefonts.com/,   http://www.dafont.com
- Use spectacular **icons** for your application main icon and for icons in the application content (menus, headers, etc.). Icons should use the PNG format, in order to be transparent.
- Here are some websites that provide great free icons: http://www.findicons.com, www.iconfinder.com, www.iconarchive.com

- Make your application dynamic: Use PUSH messages, daily news, fetch content from data sources from the web. Users will then launch your app more often.
- Share your application and content on social networks.
  Add share actions in several places of your application (header, menu, screens, etc.). Good sharing is a pre-requisite for more downloads of your app.

Useful shortcuts

Auto indent
A useful feature is Source > Correct Indentation or **Ctrl+I.** Select the code where the indents are incorrect and invoke the action. If nothing is selected, the action indents the current line.

**Quick Refactor-
Rename of a
variable**
Refactor: **Alt+Shift+T** : then Rename: **Alt+Shift+R**

Search
Search through the project: **Ctrl +H**

Debug
Step Into (**F5**), Step Over (**F6**), Run To Line (**Shift + F5**)

9. Common Tasks

Convention: local variables start with lowercase letters.

Reference the Library Project in your Android Project

From Project > Properties > Library press Add and reference the path to `<android-sdk>/extras/google/google_play_services/libproject/google-play-services_lib/`

Android Project Properties should look like this:

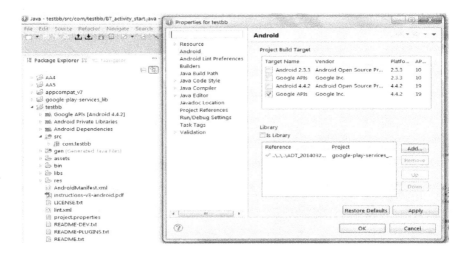

Refactoring

Refactoring is the process of transforming the code without changing its functionality. The simplest refactoring operation is renaming. However, it does require a considerable amount of work to check the code after the renaming. The standard search-and-replace function is not good to be used since every reference to the renamed object needs to be modified too. Eclipse provides more elegant solution. In order to rename a Java object, press Alt+Shift+R on Windows and Linux, or choose *Refactor>Rename* from the top menu bar. As shown below, you can rename the object, and the application code will be automatically refactored accordingly.

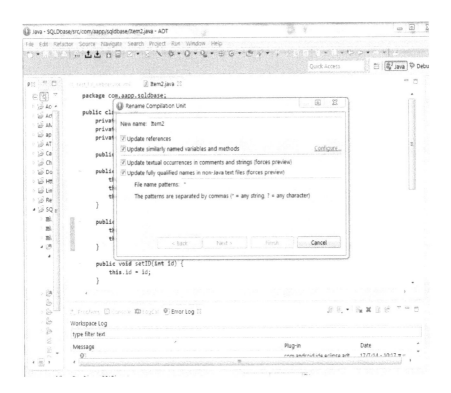

📖 Note however, that in order to rename the package name; additionally you have to change the package name in Manifest file, which is not done automatically.

Graphical Layout – Select the right Android version

When using an existing project created by somebody else you have to be sure that your ADT Graphical Layout environment correspond to the one at which the foreign environment. For example, some of the projects, supplied with this book, are written with target API 19. If you want to use the Graphical Layout environment of the projects, deselect Automatically Pick Best and select API 19.

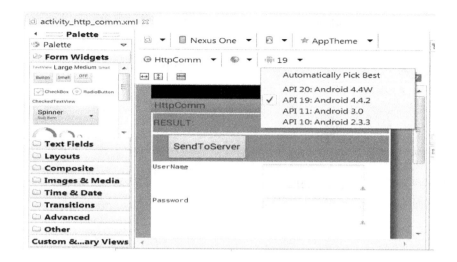

Content Assist

It is difficult to remember each type and method name of a complex project. Content Assist is a very powerful and handy tool for streamlining Android development. It is triggered by typing the dot character in the code, or it can also be manually launched by using the key combination **Ctrl+spacebar** on Windows and Linux at any time.

For example, start typing *SetContentView(* press **Ctrl+spacebar** and wait for a second. The Content Assist presents a list of suggestions to complete the current code line

```java
public class SQLDbaseActivity extends Activity {

    TextView idView;
    EditText productBox;
    EditText quantityBox;

    @Override
    protected void onCreate(Bundle savedInstanceState) {
        super.onCreate(savedInstanceState);
        setContentView(R.layout.activity_database);

        idView = (TextView) findViewById(R.id.itemID);
        productBox = (EditText) findViewById(R.id.itemName);
        quantityBox = (EditText) findViewById(R.id.itemQuantity);
    }
```

Content Assist prepares the list of the suggestions by using the first word on the left side of the cursor, and the list may be very long. In order to narrow down the suggestions, continue typing more characters, and Content Assist will filter the list accordingly.

Generate Getters and Setters

In most application development, getter and setter methods are simple but time-consuming. Eclipse's provides a useful tool for automatically creating these methods.

We will demonstrate how to use this tool to create get and set methods for Item class for Database model.

Add a new class to your project by selecting File>New>Class>Java class with Name: Item. Define the field's id, item name and quantity:

```
package com.aapp.sqldbase;
public class Item {
        private int id;
        private String itemname;
        private int quantity;

        public Item() {}

        public Item(int id, String itemname, int quantity) {
                this.id = id;
                this.itemname = itemname;
                this.quantity = quantity;
        }
}
```

After defining the fields in the class, point the cursor to class object, then select from top menu bar *Source > Generate Getters and Setters*.

This dialog provides a list of the member fields. The check box on the left side of each member field allows you to mark a field for getter and setter generation. You may expand the triangle icon to the left of the check box to select further the individual methods that will be generated. By default, both the getter and setter are generated.

Check all the fields and type OK. Eclipse generate the get and set methods of Item as described in Database model.

Use "wrap_content" and "match_parent"

To ensure that your layout is flexible and adapts to different screen sizes, you should use "wrap_content" and "match_parent" for the width and height of some view components. If you use "wrap_content", the width or height of the view is set to the minimum size necessary to fit the content within that view, while "match_parent" makes the component expand to match the size of its parent view.

By using the `"wrap_content"` and `"match_parent"` size values, instead of hard-coded sizes, your views either use only the space required for that view or expand to fill the available space, respectively.

10. Special Topics

Exchanging data between activities

When you start another activity, you may want to not only perform some actions but also exchange some information. Here we demonstrate how to launch a second activity and send to it some user-related data with different methods. The second activity displays the data received and returns back some other data to the calling activity.

Figure 35: ActivityOne screen

We make use of the Intent object to pass data between activities back and forth.

The following code snippet of code shows tree ways of sending data:

```java
package com.aapp.acivitydata;

import com.aapp.acivitydata.R;

import android.app.Activity;
import android.content.Intent;
import android.net.Uri;
import android.os.Bundle;
import android.view.View;
import android.widget.Toast;

public class ActivityOne extends Activity {

    @Override
    public void onCreate(Bundle savedInstanceState) {
        super.onCreate(savedInstanceState);
        setContentView(R.layout.activity_one);
    }

    public void onClick(View view) {
        Intent in = new Intent("SecondActivity");

        // 1. Use putExtra() method to add simple key/value pairs
        in.putExtra("Name1", "Bob");
        in.putExtra("Weight1", 75);

        // 2. Use a Bundle object to add a series of key/values
pairs
        Bundle bund = new Bundle();
        bund.putString("Name2", "Steve");
        bund.putInt("Weight2", 89);
        bund.putString("Name3", "Ronald");
        bund.putInt("Weight3", 95);

        // Attach the Bundle object to the Intent object using
putExtras()
        in.putExtras(bund);

        // 3. Use a user defined object
        UserInfo userInfo = new UserInfo();
        userInfo.setName("Alex");
        userInfo.setStreet("Atlantic");
        userInfo.setStreetNum(1242);

        // Attach the user defined object to the Intent object
        in.putExtra("userInfo", userInfo);

        // Start ActivityTwo with request code 1 waiting for
response
        startActivityForResult(in, 1);
    }

    public void onActivityResult(int requestCode, int resultCode,
Intent In)
    {
        // Check if the request code is 1
        if (requestCode == 1) {
            if (resultCode == RESULT_OK) {

                // 4. Receive data back using getData() method
                Uri url = In.getData();
                Toast.makeText(this, url.toString(),
Toast.LENGTH_SHORT).show();
            }
```

```
        }
      }
  }
}
```

First, we create an Intent object that will be attached to the second activity. We prepare three types of data to be sent. The numbers of the cases below correspond to the numbers of commented lines in the code:

1. To send primitive data types (key/value pairs) we use the putExtra() method:

```
in.putExtra("Name1", "Bob");
in.putExtra("Weight1", 75);
```

(one string-valued [Name1: "Bob"] and one integer-valued pair [Weight1: 75])

2. We use a Bundle object to add a series of key/values pairs: [Name2: "Steve"], [Weight2: 75], [Name3: "Ronald"], [Weight3: 95]). It is attached to the bundle via putExtras() method.
3. To send user defined object we create an instance of it, assign values to it and then attached it to the bundle via putExtra() method.

When we start another activity using the Intent object, the data attached to it is passed to the destination activity. We use the startActivityForResult() method to get some data back from it. The startActivityForResult() method takes an Intent object and a request code which is a positive integer. It identifies returning activities, as you may call more than one activity. If the request code is -1, then the call of startActivityForResult() is equivalent to startActivity(), i.e. no data passed back from the destination activity.

Let us see what happens on the target activity (see the code below):

```java
package com.aapp.acivitydata;

import com.aapp.acivitydata.R;

import android.app.Activity;
import android.content.Intent;
import android.net.Uri;
import android.os.Bundle;
import android.view.View;
import android.widget.Toast;

public class ActivityTwo extends Activity {
    @Override
    public void onCreate(Bundle savedInstanceState) {
        super.onCreate(savedInstanceState);
        setContentView(R.layout.activity_two);

        // 1. Receive data from ActivityOne:
        //       using getStringExtra()
        Toast.makeText(this,getIntent().getStringExtra("Name1"),
            Toast.LENGTH_SHORT).show();
        //       using getIntExtra()

Toast.makeText(this,Integer.toString(getIntent().getIntExtra("Wei
ght1", 0)),
            Toast.LENGTH_SHORT).show();

        // 2. Receive Bundle object from ActivityOne
        Bundle bundle = getIntent().getExtras();
        //       Receive data from bundle object:
        //       using the getString()
        Toast.makeText(this, bundle.getString("Name2"),
Toast.LENGTH_SHORT).show();
        //       using the getInt()

Toast.makeText(this,Integer.toString(bundle.getInt("Weight2")),
                        Toast.LENGTH_SHORT).show();
        Toast.makeText(this, bundle.getString("Name3"),
                        Toast.LENGTH_SHORT).show();

Toast.makeText(this,Integer.toString(bundle.getInt("Weight3")),
                        Toast.LENGTH_SHORT).show();

        // 3. Receive custom defined object from ActivityOne
        UserInfo usinf = (UserInfo)
getIntent().getSerializableExtra("userInfo");
        Toast.makeText(this, usinf.Name(),
Toast.LENGTH_SHORT).show();
        Toast.makeText(this, usinf.Street(),
Toast.LENGTH_SHORT).show();
        Toast.makeText(this, Integer.toString(usinf.StreetNum()),
                        Toast.LENGTH_SHORT).show();
```

```
    }

    public void onClick(View view) {
        // Create an Intent object to return data:
        Intent in = new Intent();

        // 4. Return data using the setData() method
        in.setData(Uri.parse("http://www.test.com"));

        setResult(RESULT_OK, in);

        finish();
    }
}
```

To retrieve the data that was passed to the second activity, we use the getIntent() method to obtain the instance of the Intent object that was passed to it. To get the three types of data passed we use:

1. get<type>Extra method, where the type may be Int, String, etc. It corresponds to putExtra() method, used in the calling activity.
2. To receive Bundle object from calling activity we use getExtras() method to retrieve a series of key/values pairs.
3. Finally, to retrieve a user defined object from calling activity, we use getSerializableExtra() method
4. The destination may also pass data back to the calling activity creating another Intent object. You can set the values as described earlier. Here we show the use of another method - setResult(RESULT_OK, in) to pass an Uri object back. The first parameter indicates to the calling activity whether the data returned should be ignored or not (RESULT_CANCELLED or RESULT_OK). The second parameter is the Intent object.

Back in the calling ActivityOne, see the implementation of onActivityResult() method (// 4. Receive data back):

Here we check the request code to ensure that we are getting the result from the correct activity. This is the number 1, that we earlier passed to the startActivityForResult(i, 1) method. We also check the result code to see if it is RESULT_OK: To retrieve the data sent using the setData() method, we use the getData() method of the Intent object, passed in as the third argument of the onActivityResult() method.

In order to create the complete project and run it, create a Skeleton project named ActivityData with package name **com.aapp.acivitydata.** Add the two previous classes. In addition, you need to add UserInfo class:

```java
package com.aapp.acivitydata;
import java.io.Serializable;
public class UserInfo implements Serializable {
    private static final long serialVersionUID = 1L;
    String Name;
    String Street;
    int    StreetNum;

    public void setName(String Name) {
        this.Name = Name;
    }

    public String Name() {
        return Name;
    }

    public void setStreet(String Street) {
        this.Street = Street;
    }

    public String Street() {
        return Street;
    }

    public void setStreetNum(int StreetNum) {
        this.StreetNum = StreetNum;
    }

    public int StreetNum() {
        return StreetNum;
    }
}
```

Add to res/layout: **activity_one.xml**

```
<RelativeLayout
 xmlns:android="http://schemas.android.com/apk/res/android"
    xmlns:tools="http://schemas.android.com/tools"
    android:layout_width="match_parent"
    android:layout_height="match_parent" >

    <Button
        android:id="@+id/button1"
        android:layout_width="wrap_content"
        android:layout_height="wrap_content"
        android:layout_centerHorizontal="true"
        android:layout_centerVertical="true"
        android:text="Go to Activity Two"
        android:onClick="onClick" />

    <TextView
        android:id="@+id/textView1"
        android:layout_width="wrap_content"
        android:layout_height="wrap_content"
        android:layout_above="@+id/button1"
        android:layout_centerHorizontal="true"
        android:layout_marginBottom="62dp"
        android:text="Activity One"

android:textAppearance="?android:attr/textAppearanceMedium" />
</RelativeLayout>
```

and **activity_two.xml:**

```
<RelativeLayout
 xmlns:android="http://schemas.android.com/apk/res/android"
    xmlns:tools="http://schemas.android.com/tools"
    android:layout_width="match_parent"
    android:layout_height="match_parent" >

    <Button
        android:id="@+id/button1"
        android:layout_width="wrap_content"
        android:layout_height="wrap_content"
        android:layout_centerHorizontal="true"
        android:layout_centerVertical="true"
        android:text="Back to Activity One"
        android:onClick="onClick" />

    <TextView
        android:id="@+id/textView1"
        android:layout_width="wrap_content"
        android:layout_height="wrap_content"
        android:layout_above="@+id/button1"
        android:layout_centerHorizontal="true"
        android:layout_marginBottom="92dp"
        android:text="Activity Two"

android:textAppearance="?android:attr/textAppearanceMedium" />
</RelativeLayout>
```

The res/values/strings.xml is:

```
<resources>
    <string name="app_name">ActivityData</string>
    <string name="title_activity_one">ActivityOne</string>
    <string name="title_activity_two">ActivityTwo</string>
</resources>
```

The AndroidManifest.xml is:

```
<manifest
xmlns:android="http://schemas.android.com/apk/res/android"
    package="com.aapp.acivitydata"
    android:versionCode="1"
    android:versionName="1.0" >

    <uses-sdk
        android:minSdkVersion="8"
        android:targetSdkVersion="15" />

    <application
        android:icon="@drawable/ic_launcher"
        android:label="@string/app_name"
        android:theme="@style/AppTheme" >
        <activity
            android:name="com.aapp.acivitydata.ActivityOne"
            android:label="@string/title_activity_one" >
            <intent-filter>
                <action android:name="android.intent.action.MAIN"
/>
                <category
android:name="android.intent.category.LAUNCHER" />
            </intent-filter>

        </activity>
        <activity
            android:name="com.aapp.acivitydata.ActivityTwo"
            android:label="@string/title_activity_two" >
            <intent-filter>
                <action android:name="SecondActivity" />
                <category
android:name="android.intent.category.DEFAULT" />
            </intent-filter>
        </activity>
    </application>
</manifest>
```

Convert HTML5 into standalone Android Application

Create an Android app using Eclipse.

Create a layout that has a <WebView> control:

To add a **WebView** to your Application, simply include the **WebView** element in your activity layout. For example, here is a layout file in which the **WebView** fills the screen:

```xml
<?xml version="1.0" encoding="utf-8"?>
<WebView
 xmlns:android="http://schemas.android.com/apk/res/android"
    android:id="@+id/webview"
    android:layout_width="fill_parent"
    android:layout_height="fill_parent"
/>
```

To load a web page in the **WebView**, use loadUrl(). For example:

```java
WebView myWebView = (WebView) findViewById(R.id.webview);
myWebView.loadUrl("http://www.example.com");
```

Before this will work, however, your application must have access to the Internet. To get Internet access, request the INTERNET permission in your manifest file. For example:

```xml
<manifest ... >
    <uses-permission android:name="android.permission.INTERNET"
/>
    ...
</manifest>
```

Move your HTML code to **/assets** folder and load it with **WebView** .

Now you have an android app.

AVD – telnet access

Each emulator instance is automatically assigned a unique port number between 5554 and 5584. This number appears before the configuration name on the title bar of the emulator window. The emulator listens on that port number to provide access to the Android console.

A telnet application (e.g. Putty) can be used to connect to that port to access the Android console and interact with the remote service. Using the telnet connect to localhost and the port number. After you have connected to the Android console, the text-based interface allows you to control the emulator and the hardware features. By typing help, you can get a list the available commands, as shown in the following screenshot:

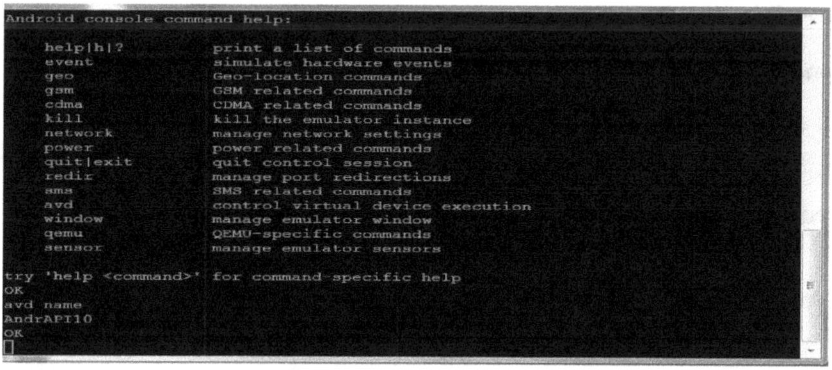

Figure 36: AVD telnet access

Install and test APK manually on simulator

If you only have a binary .APK created from other environment and do not have the project that creates it (e.g. created on application builders), you still can install and test it on the emulator without using ADT environment. There is a tool **adb** (short for Android Debug Bridge), that is included in the Android SDK we installed earlier and can be used for that purpose. To do so, do the following:

1. Add the path of <android_sdk>/platform-tools to environment variable PATH, if you have not already added it.
2. Start an emulator from ADT or manually (e.g., for MakeMeDroid_Emulator start emulator.bat).
3. Open a command line window (cmd) and list the running devices with the command   **adb devices**
4. Install your app with the following command (replacing *<file-location>***app_name.apk** with the actual location of the .APK file):

adb -e install -r <file-location>app_name.apk

The **-e** flag tells adb to install our binary package (i.e., *<file-location>test.apk*) on the first running emulator that it finds. The **-r** flag tells **adb** to replace the binary on the emulator if it has been installed previously. If you get a "device offline" error, go into the emulator and unlock it if it is locked then try again.

5. Go to emulator, press Application icon (white square dotted icon), and scroll to find your app and run it.

11. Debugging

The Android SDK has a built-in Java debugger and a good monitoring tool DDMS (named by Dalvik Debug Monitor Server). You can use both the debugger, along with DDMS, to debug your applications. ADT displays the debugger and DDMS features as perspectives, which are customized views that display certain tabs and windows depending on the perspective that you are in. Eclipse also takes care of starting the ADB host daemon for you, so you do not have to run this manually.

The Debug Perspective in Eclipse

- The Debug Perspective in Eclipse gives you access to the following tabs:
- Debug - Displays previously and currently debugged Android applications and its currently running threads
- Variables - When breakpoints are set, displays variable values during code execution
- Breakpoints - Displays a list of the set breakpoints in your application code
- LogCat - Allows you to view system log messages in real time. The LogCat tab is also available in the DDMS perspective.

Here we will demonstrate how to debug MetricConverter project:

Open the project. In ConvertMetricActivity.java locate `private double EUtoUS(double inpVal)` and put a break-point (`Ctl+Shift+B`) on line: `switch (iRadioBtn) {`

From Top Menu select Run>Debug (F11). An instance of MetricConverter starts, then put some value in Meter (m) field (e.g. 88) and press Convert button. At that moment, you enter the break point and the execution of the application stops waiting for you to debug step-by-step.

- Access the Debug Perspective by clicking Window > Open Perspective > Debug.

You should see something like:

🖳 *Figure 37: Debug Perspective*

At top-left (Debug) window you see application threads. At top-right
(Variables) window you see all active variables are displayed. In this case
a pointer (this) to the ConvertMetricActivity class outVal and inpVal,
which holds the last value we entered (88.0). The middle-left window is
the source-code window and shows the line we have reached during the
execution (**switch (iRadioBtn)**). Now from Top Menu Run window we

have different choices to proceed:

```
Step Into                              F5
Step Over                              F6
Step Return                            F7
Run to Line                         Ctrl+R
Use Step Filters                   Shift+F5
Run                                Ctrl+F11
Debug                                 F11
Run History                             ▶
Run As                                  ▶
Run Configurations...
Debug History                           ▶
Debug As                                ▶
Debug Configurations...
Toggle Breakpoint               Ctrl+Shift+B
Toggle Line Breakpoint
Toggle Method Breakpoint
```

Step Into (**F5**), Step Over (**F6**), Run To Line (**Shift + F5**), etc.

For example, press several times **F6** in order to proceed line by line.

Debugging with DDMS

DDMS allows developers to monitor and interact with attached devices and emulators. It provides access to process and thread states, heap information, a file explorer, logs, port forwarding, screen capture and many other features. DDMS also acts as a bridge between the Dalvik virtual machine running on the device or emulator, as well as the debugger. It handles the lower-level communication setup to allow the Eclipse debugger to communicate with the Dalvik virtual machine. This allows developers to debug Android applications easily, as if they were plain Java applications running on the host machine. ADT represents DDMS with multiple screen views.

The DDMS Perspective lets you access all of the features of DDMS from within the IDE. The following sections of DDMS are available to you:

- Devices - Shows the list of devices and AVDs that are connected to ADB.
- Emulator Control - Lets you carry out device functions.

- LogCat - Lets you view system log messages in real time.

- Threads - Shows currently running threads within a VM.

- Heap - Shows heap usage for a VM.

- Allocation Tracker - Shows the memory allocation of objects.

- File Explorer - Lets you explore the device's file system.

To launch it, select Window->Open Perspective> Other from the top menu bar and select DDMS from the Open Perspective dialog.

Here is an example of monitoring pre-loaded thread for Metric Converter running instance:

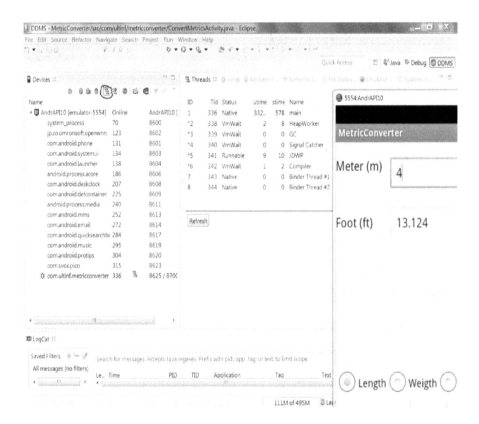

Figure 38: DDMS Perspective

Note: In order to activate the threads in the right window you first have to refresh the threads icon circled in blue on the top left icons row.

How to decompile .dex into .java source code

There are two alternatives, depending on what you want to accomplish:

- Decompile the Dalvik byte code (dex) into readable Java source. You can do this easily with dex2jar and jd-gui. The resulting source is useful to read and understand the functionality of an app, but will likely not produce 100% usable code. In other words, you can read the source, but you cannot really modify and repackage it. Note that if the source has been obfuscated with proguard, the resulting source code will be substantially more difficult to untangle.

- For example, let's take **TxtSpeak.apk** from TextToSpeech project (it can be found in /bin directory of the project) and see how it could be converted with these two utilities:

  o **dex2jar**

(For more info, see

https://code.google.com/p/dex2jar/wiki/ModifyApkWithDexTool)

\# convert classes.dex in TxtSpeak.apk to TxtSpeak_dex2jar.jar
d2j-dex2jar.bat -f -o TxtSpeak_dex2jar.jar TxtSpeak.apk
\# verify jar
d2j-asm-verify.bat TxtSpeak_dex2jar.jar

convert to jasmin format

d2j-jar2jasmin.bat -f -o TxtSpeak_jasmin TxtSpeak_dex2jar.jar

- o **gd-gui**

- Open with JD-GUI TxtSpeak_dex2jar.jar
- Save > All Sources => saves to TxtSpeak_dex2jar.src.zip
- Unzip it to some dir and you have all *.j files converted to readable *.java files
- The other major alternative is to disassemble the byte code to *smali*, an assembly language designed for precisely this purpose. The easiest way to do this is with apktool. Once you have got apktool installed, you can just point it at an apk file, and you will get back a smali file for each class contained in the application. You can read and modify the smali or even replace classes entirely by generating smali from new Java source.
- You may download apktool from:

  https://code.google.com/p/android-apktool/downloads/list

  and smalli from:

  https://bitbucket.org/JesusFreke/smali/downloads

- Let us use for example the same .apk:
- java -jar apktool_2.0.0b9.jar d TxtSpeak.apk
- This generates the TxtSpeak directory that contains Readable resources (\res) and smali files.
- Then you may use:

  http://sourceforge.net/projects/jasmin/files/

- to transform smali files to Java.

12. Installation and updates of ADT components

Installation Details

To check all installation details (Software, Features, Configuration, etc.) select:

Help > About Eclipse(ADT) > Installation Details. E.g. to see installed plugins, select Plug-in tab:

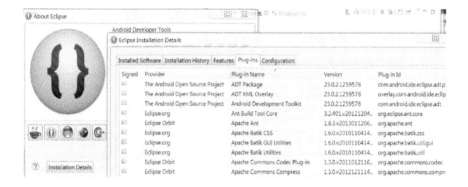

Updating ADT

- Select from the top most tab: Help > Install New Software and Click **Add**, in the top-right corner.
- In the Add Repository dialog that appears, enter "ADT Plugin" for the Name and the following URL for the Location: https://dl-ssl.google.com/android/eclipse/   Click **OK.**

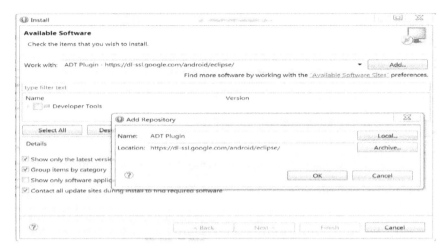

📖 *Figure 39: Add Repository dialog*

- In the Available Software dialog, select the checkbox next to Developer Tools and click **Next**.

- In the next window, you will see a list of the tools to be downloaded. Select them all and Click **Next**.

For example, to install **ADT Translation Manager Plugin** follow the steps as described above, then:

- In the Add Repository dialog that appears, enter a repository name for the Name and the following URL for the Location **https**://dl.google.com/alt/

- Click **OK**.

- In the Available Software dialog, select the checkbox next to **Android Developer Tools - Translation Manager** and click **Next**.

13. Free Application Builders

If you don't want to invest time and effort in learning and developing you may choose to use application builders. With these application builders, you may build mobile app in few minutes. No special programming skills are required. Even you have programming skills it is helpful to compare your design with the one provided by these application builders. Here we describe a few free application builders that can be found on internet.

Creating fast Android applications with MakeMeDroid

The concept of Make Me Droid is to use template screens that you fill with your data. They can be linked together to create the application flow, starting with a main screen. You can customize those screens, or build your screens from nothing.

How to create a test application:

Create free account on http://www.makemedroid.com/

Go to *My Applications* > *New application* at the left panel.

Select: *Application Style, Design and Settings, Application elements*.

Then select *Android* tab.

From the right panel put app version, next press "*Generate the Application*" button.

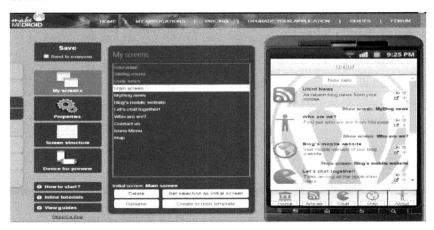

💻 *Figure 40: Generate Application - MakeMeDroid*

You may try the application on Android simulator, or download it and test it on a mobile device.

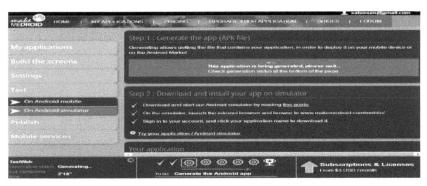

💻 *Figure 41: APK ready for download - MakeMeDroid*

Start an emulator

Download the emulator from:

http://www.makemedroid.com/getfile.php?t=emu&f=MakeMeDroid_Android_Emulator_v2.zip

Unzip it and start the emulator from supplied .bat file **Make me Droid -
Android 2.3 emulator.bat** or start one from AVD manager in Eclipse.
Install and run the .APK binary as it is described in <u>Install and test APK
manually on simulator</u>.

Ready to publish it on Google Play:

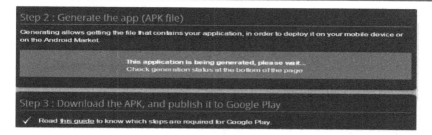

You may publish your app on Google Play, but first you have to take
some screenshots, required by Google Play:

Getting Application Screenshots

- From the application, go to the screen from which you want to
  get a screenshot. Press the **menu** key of your phone, and
  then **Take screenshot**.

- The screenshot will be sent to Make me Droid online storage, as
  a form. Check your forms on the website, going to **mobile
  services** then **dynamic application content**.

🖳 *Figure 42: Saved Screenshots- MakeMeDroid*

QR code generator

This useful tool lets you generate a QR code for your Android application:

http://www.makemedroid.com/en/qr/

A QR code allows storing internet addresses but also other kind of information. Adding your Android application QR code to your own website lets mobile devices access your application Android market page using a QR code scanner. Here is an example of my website QR code, **generated by this tool:**

📖 *Figure 43: MakeMeDroid – QR code generator*

The generated QR code is at the bottom – right side.

Adding QR Code to your app

Select from left panel App > Mobile Services, then from right panel Dynamic Application Content > Application forms > Add. Put form name, id_name, select format > picture and upload QR_code.jpg.

📖 *Figure 44: MakeMeDroid – Addig QR code to app*

If you own a WordPress blog and you want to create its pair mobile application. You just have to make a Make me Droid application, and also show some of your blog content in it. For more details check:

http://www.makemedroid.com/en/guides/wordpressconnect/

Creating fast Android application with BuzzTouch

Create an account at https://www.buzztouch.com/

How to download your buzztouch Project

Expand the "Choose Plugins to Include" section and pick the plugins you want to include with your project. At the very minimum, you will need to include the "required" plugins, which are ones for screens you have configured in your control panel. If there are screen types, you think you will use in the future, select those plugins as well, so you do not have to download the project again later. Remember, these plugins define what your app is capable of doing. If there is some functionality, you think you might want to add in a future version of the app, it would be a good idea to select that plugin now. Then all you need to do is configure that screen in your control panel, and the code will be there ready and waiting for you. No need to download the package a second time. Avoid selecting them all…that increases the size of your app, and there is no reason to do that if you do not have to (and plenty of reasons to avoid it).

Figure 45: BuzzTouch app builder

Import your Android application into Eclipse Launch the Eclipse development environment. When Eclipse loads, you could see any number of views or panels. Eclipse refers to these views as Perspectives. Customizing your Perspective in the Eclipse IDE (Integrated Development Environment) is common. When Eclipse is finished

launching, use the menu toolbar and select: **File > Import > Android >
Existing Android Code Into Workspace**

Creating fast Android application with AppyPie

Sign up at http://www.appypie.com/

Choose subscription plan from http://www.appypie.com/pricing-
plan. There is also a free one.

From Dashboard menu, you may create and edit your apps.

Figure 46: AppyPie dashboard

14. Prepare your app for publishing on Google Play

Create a private key:

Android applications must be signed before they can be installed on an
Android device. During development phase, Eclipse signs your
application automatically with a debug key.

In order to prepare your application for publishing on Google Play you have to sign it in Release mode:

Using Package Explorer, choose the application project, right-click it, and choose *Android Tools->Export Signed Application Package* from the context menu to launch the Export Android Application wizard

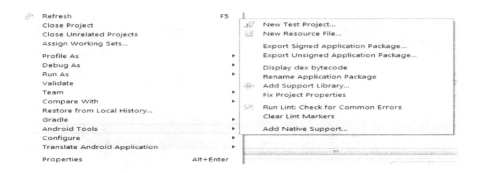

Figure 47: Selecting Export Android Application

From context menu, select Export Android Application:

📖 *Figure 48: Export Android Application wizard*

This wizard allows to use an existing key or to create a new one. Make sure to back up your key.

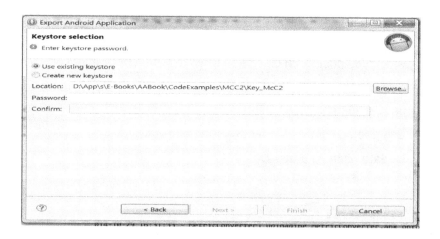

📖 *Figure 49: Key Store of Export Android Application wizard*

It also do zip align, which is required for publishing on Google Play.

You need to use the same signature key in Google Play to update your application. If you lose the key, **you will not be able to update your application ever again!**

Upload your signed binary to Google Play.

You need to be a registered Android Developer to upload your app. If have not already registered, you can do so at *http://market.android.com/publish/signup*. The process is quick and easy—you just fill out a bit of profile information (name, email, phone, etc.), pay a $25 registration fee (using Google Checkout), and agree to the Android Market Developer Distribution Agreement.

- Launch your web browser, navigate to http://market.android.com/publish/ and sign in to your Google account.

- If you aren't forwarded automatically after logging in, navigate to http://market.android.com/publish/Home and click the Upload Application button

- When you publish on Google Play, write a **description** that is long enough, interesting, and that contains keywords that users usually search.

- Use good quality and attractive **screenshots**.

- **Update** often your application.

15. Common Errors:

A. Emulator PANIC: Could not open AVD

AVD is looking for files on C:\USERS\XXX\.android\avd. If it cannot be found, create a new environment variable: ANDROID_SDK_HOME to point to the directory containing your .android directory. The emulator and SDK Manager will pick it up properly.

B. Eclipse Error: Failed to create the Java Virtual Machine

Figure 50: Eclipse Error - No Java VM

Add the path of Java VM to your PATH system variable: e.g. append to PATH:

";C:\Program Files\Java\jre7\bin" or

Select Start menu > Computer > System Properties > Advanced System Properties. Then open Advanced tab > Environment Variables and add a new system variable JAVA_HOME that points to your JDK folder, for example **C:\Program Files\Java\jdk1.7.0_21**.

C. Android SDK Manager: No possibility to create new activity

After updating SDK tools, the possibility to create new Activity is lost:

Cntl+N > Android > Android Application Project > Create new project. => The src folder is empty

After updating Android SDK Tool by latest 22.6 version, an update of DDMS Tools and Plugins is required (see underlined ADT), which is not mentioned or done by SDK Manager.

Go to *Help Menu > Install New software* and install from URL:

https://dl-ssl.google.com/android/eclipse/

Update to **"Devloper Tools"** and **"NDK Plugins"** by latest Version.

🖳 *Figure 51: NDK Pluggins*

Follow default screens by pressing **Next** button.

D. Android Virtual Device Manager: The existing devices don't work

After updating SDK tools from ADT 22.3 to 22.6 the possibility to create new virtual devices was lost.

Starting an AVD from ADT results in Error: Unhandled event loop exception.

RESOLUTION:

Run the AVD Manager with admin rights: start it outside from ADT and create your virtual devices there.

E. Failed to load properties file for project

```
eclipse.buildId=v22.3.0-887826
java.version=1.7.0_51
java.vendor=Oracle Corporation
BootLoader constants: OS=win32, ARCH=x86, WS=win32,
NL=en_US
Framework arguments:  -product
com.android.ide.eclipse.adt.package.product
Command-line arguments:  -os win32 -ws win32 -arch x86 -
product com.android.ide.eclipse.adt.package.product

Error: Failed to load properties file for project
'TestLG3'
```

RESOLUTION:

- Go to Window -> Android SDK Manager
- It automatically shows the new packages/updates to existing packages. Packages are grouped by API Level.
- Go to the required API - Level group and you will find an option "Sources for Android SDK" checkbox. Select this check box and click on 'Install Packages' button. You may want to un-select the packages that you do not need.
- Now the source code is downloaded to //sources/ folder.
- Open any Android class in the Eclipse editor and it now asks for the source path. Give the source path as //sources/.

F. Call requires API level N2 (current min is n=N1): <specific line>

RESOLUTION:

In AndroidManifest.xml edit/add the min/target SDK version, e.g.:

```
<uses-sdk
    android:minSdkVersion="8"
```

```
android:targetSdkVersion="19" />
```

G. "Using 1.7 requires compiling with Android 4.4 (KitKat); currently using API 10".

RESOLUTION:

- Install Java JRE 6.
- In Preferences>Java>Installed JRE>Add>Standard VM **Add** the path to JRE6.

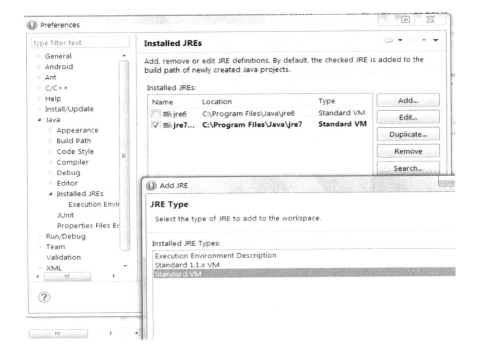

Figure 52: Different API

- Right click on your Project > Properties > Java compiler > enable "project specific settings".
- Set Compiler compliance level to 1.6 and rebuild your project

H. R cannot be resolved to a variable

Cause: gen/R.java is missing!

Project > Clean   should re-create it.

If it is not created, try the following:

- Add the following import to project in order to get access to the <package> resources: import <package>.R;
- If it is not resolved, check for some other errors in resources and fix them, then "clean" again.

I. Unable to resolve target 'android' <N>

You can right click on your Project > Properties > Android > Select the Target android version you want to compile and Apply!

If you do not have any target versions to compile, you probably need to download them on your SDK Manager

J. Android emulator: No command output when running: 'am start'

In Eclipse, Increase the ADB connection timeout by following below steps:

- **Window > Preferences**

- Select **Andriod > DDMS** from left panel
- Increase value of "**ADB connection time out (ms)**"

K. "Unexpected namespace prefix "xmlns" found for tag..."

RESOLUTION:

Go to the Project > Clean. Select current project from the list and Click Ok. All the XMLNS errors should have been resolved.

This should be tried before trying any other solution! This is like restarting the system for Window's error that resolves problems more of the times.

L. Basic4Android: " Cannot find: \Android\SDK\tools\platform-tools\aapt.exe"

RESOLUTION:

Copy lib and to aapt.exe from <ADT_SDK>\sdk\build-tools\<vers.num> to <ADT_SDK>\platform-tools.

M. Eclipse > Run: "your project contains errors...", but no errors seen

RESOLUTION:

That usually comes from errors in the build path. In Eclipse, there is a view that lists all the errors called "Problems". Add that view by: Window > Show View > Problems.

N. Eclipse > "Error retrieving parent for item"

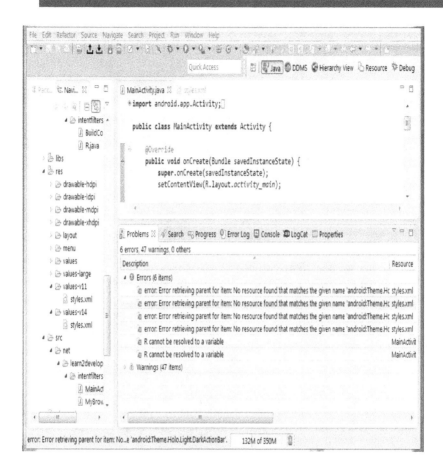

📖 *Figure 53: Error retrieving parent for item*

This is one of the most typical cases, where you refer to the Holo theme as

```
parent = "@android:style/Theme.Holo".
```

To use the Holo theme you have to set the build target in your manifest to API level 11 or later, also you have to put the `style.xml` file containing the Holo theme to the folder `values-v11`.

The easiest resolution is to remove the Holo theme from style.xml. In this way, you do not have to change API level. See also Refactor a project without appcompat.

O. HAXM speeds up the slow Android Emulator

RESOLUTION:

If your computer support Intel VirtualizationTechnology (check your BIOS features) you may use HAXM Driver to create an x86 AVD, which is much faster. HAXM stands for - "Intel Hardware Accelerated Execution Manager"

- Install the HAXM Driver by running "IntelHaxm.exe".
  It will be located in
  `<sdk>\extras\intel\Hardware_Accelerated_Execution_`
  `Manager`
- If the installer fails with message that Intel VT must be turned on, you need to enable this in BIOS.
- Create a New x86 AVD: Follow the image below:

Figure 54: Intel Hardware Accelerated AVD

- From Emulation Options select: <u>Use Host GPU</u>

P. Eclipse error: "Multiple dex files define"

If you get Dex Load Error: Unable to execute dex: Multiple dex files define

Select *Project > Right Click > Select Build Path > Configure Build Path >*

In Libraries tab, remove Android Dependencies -> OK. Then clean the project and run again.

16. Questions and Answers

A. What is URI?

Short for Uniform Resource Identifier, the generic term for all types of names and addresses that refer to objects on the World Wide Web. A URL is one kind of URI.

B. How to access Internet from emulator?

If you use Internet with a proxy, you will not be able to access it from AVD emulator unless you add the following configuration settings:

On Project > Run As > Run Configuration> Android Application > App > Target > Additional Emulator Command Line Options add the proxy settings: -http-proxy http://xx.xxx.xx.xx:8080

In addition, you may try `'username:password@proxy:port'`

🖥 *Figure 55: Proxy for Emulators*

Alternatively:

At *Window > Prefferences > Android > Launch add –http-proxy* settings:

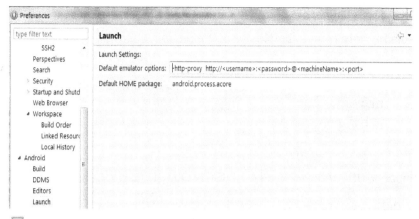

Figure 56: Proxy for Emulators from Prefferences > Android

C. What is smali?

Smali is a readable form of Android bytecode. It can be called decompilation language of Android bytecode. Android application package, apk or jar, can be decompiled to smali by <u>baksmali</u> or <u>apktool</u>.

smali2java is a tool that can decompile smali to java sources.

D. What is JSON?

JSON stands for JavaScript Object Notation. It's a lightweight data interchange format. The notation is easy for humans to read and write and easy for machines to parse and generate. In short, a JSON object is a list of Key-Value pairs or JSON objects.

A Key-Value pair consists of two entities separated by colons (:). Value can be a string, a number, a sub-object or a list.

For example: { **"name"** : " **Lyza"** } is a Key-Value pair, where **"name"** is Key and **"Lyza"** is Value. This is a simple JSON object. It is denoted by curly brackets { }.

A list consists of items separated by comas and is enclosed by square brackets [ ]. Here is an example of Key-Value pair where Value is a list:

```
"cc" : [
        "fm@gmail.com",
        "glob@alpha.com"
    ]
```

A compound JSON object is a list of JSON Objects. Let us see an example:

```
{
"name" : " Lyza",
"email" : "ly@milla.com",
"id" : 1517,
"real_name" : "Lyza Bell",
"picture: "Lyza.bmp",
"cc" : [
            "fm@gmail.com",
            "glob@alpha.com"
        ],
"cc_detail" : [
            {
                "email" : "fm@gmail.com",
                "id" : 3676,
                "real_name" : "Forge (fmdevel)"
            },
            {
                "email" : "glob@alpha.com",
                "id" : 1364,
                "real_name" : "Teddy"
            }
        ],
"tasks" : [task1, task2],
"depends_on" : [task11, task12, task21,task22, task23],
"due_date" :  "2015-11-08"
}
```

In this example, our JSON is an object (denoted by {...}) containing simple Key-Value pairs name, email, id, real name, picture, due_date, Key-Value pairs with a cc: [...] list of email addresses, tasks: [...] and depends_on:[...] tasks and a Key-Value pair with a list of JSON objects cc_detail : [{...}, {...}].

Android Release Versions, Codenames and API Levels

Android versions have been developed under a **confectionery**-themed **code name** and released in alphabetical order:

```
Android 1.0                              (API level 1)
Android 1.1                              (API level 2)
Android 1.5        Cupcake               (API level 3)
Android 1.6        Donut                 (API level 4)
Android 2.0        Eclair                (API level 5)
Android 2.0.1      Eclair                (API level 6)
Android 2.1        Eclair                (API level 7)
Android 2.2-2.2.3  Froyo                 (API level 8)
Android 2.3-2.3.2  Gingerbread           (API level 9)
Android 2.3.3-2.3.7 Gingerbread          (API level 10)
Android 3.0        Honeycomb             (API level 11)
Android 3.1        Honeycomb             (API level 12)
Android 3.2        Honeycomb             (API level 13)
Android 4.0-4.0.2  Ice Cream Sandwich    (API level 14)
Android 4.0.3-4.0.4 Ice Cream Sandwich   (API level 15)
Android 4.1        Jelly Bean            (API level 16)
Android 4.2        Jelly Bean            (API level 17)
Android 4.3        Jelly Bean            (API level 18)
Android 4.4.2      KitKat                (API level 19)
Android 4.4W                             (API level 20)
Android L          L                     (API level 20)
```

Table: Android Release Versions, Codenames and API Levels

As it is seen, there are 20 API levels that you should consider while developing your applications. The API level determines the size of your audience as well, so picking this number wisely is very important while developing a new Android application. Google announced that more than1 billion activated devices now use the Android OS worldwide.

By selecting min API level **8,** you are targeting **95**% of devices.

Useful sites, downloads:

Developer sites

http://developer.android.com/

http://developer.android.com/training/

http://developer.android.com/design/downloads/index.html

Facebook developers:
https://developers.facebook.com/docs/android/getting-started/

SDK

Download SDK: https://developers.facebook.com/docs/android/

Rapid Application Development (RAD) tools:

Basic4Android: http://www.basic4ppc.com/

17. Index

www.ingramcontent.com/pod-product-compliance
Lightning Source LLC
Chambersburg PA
CBHW071200050326

40689CB00011B/2189